SHAKESPEARE'S POLITICS

Allan Bloom with Harry V. Jaffa

The University of Chicago Press
Chicago and London

This edition is published by arrangement with
Basic Books, Inc.

The University of Chicago Press, Chicago 60637
The University of Chicago Press, Ltd., London

©1964 by Basic Books, Inc.
All rights reserved. Published 1964
University of Chicago Press edition 1981
Printed in the United States of America
01 00   4 5 6 7 8

Library of Congress Cataloging in Publication Data

Bloom, Allan David, 1930–
Shakespeare's politics.

Includes bibliographical references and index.
1. Shakespeare, William, 1564–1616—Political and social views. 2. Politics in
literature.
I. Jaffa, Harry V. II. Title.
PR3017.B55   1981   822.3'3   81–10342
ISBN 0-226-06041-1   AACR2

⊗ The paper used in this publication meets the minimum requirements of the
American National Standard for Information Sciences—Permanence of Paper for
Printed Library Materials, ANSI Z39.48—1984.

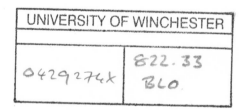

TO

Leo Strauss

OUR TEACHER

Contents

SHAKESPEARE'S POLITICS

I

Political Philosophy and Poetry

◦§ INTRODUCTION §◦

I

THE MOST striking fact about contemporary university students is that there is no longer any canon of books which forms their taste and their imagination. In general, they do not look at all to books when they meet problems in life or try to think about their goals; there are no literary models for their conceptions of virtue and vice. This state of affairs itself reflects the deeper fact of the decay of the common understanding of—and agreement on—first principles that is characteristic of our times. The role once played by the Bible and Shakespeare in the education of the English-speaking peoples is now largely played by popular journalism or the works of ephemeral authors. This does not mean that the classic authors are no longer read; they are perhaps read more and in greater variety than ever before. But they do not move; they do not seem to speak to the situation of the modern young; they are not a part of the furniture of the student's mind, once he is out of the academic atmosphere.

This results in a decided lowering of tone in their reflections on life and its goals; today's students are technically well-equipped, but Philistine.

The civilizing and unifying function of the peoples' books, which was carried out in Greece by Homer, Italy by Dante, France by Racine and Molière, and Germany by Goethe, seems to be dying a rapid death. The young have no ground from which to begin their understanding of the world and themselves, and they have no common education which forms the core of their communication with their fellows. A Marlborough could once say that he had formed his understanding of English history from Shakespeare alone; such a reliance on a poet today is almost inconceivable. The constant return to and reliance on a single great book or author has disappeared, and the result is not only a vulgarization of the tone of life but an atomization of society, for a civilized people is held together by its common understanding of what is virtuous and vicious, noble and base.

Shakespeare could still be the source of such an education and provide the necessary lessons concerning human virtue and the proper aspirations of a noble life. He is respected in our tradition, and he is of our language. But the mere possession of his works is not enough; they must be properly read and interpreted. One could never re-establish the Mosaic religion on the basis of a Bible read by the Higher Critics, nor could one use Shakespeare as a text in moral and political education on the basis of his plays as they are read by the New Critics.

There has been a change in the understanding of the nature of poetry since the rise of the Romantic movement, and it is now considered a defiling of art's sacred temple to see the poem as a mirror of nature or to interpret it as actually *teaching* something. Poets are believed not to have had intentions, and their epics and dramas are said to be *sui generis*, not to be judged by the standards of civil society or of religion. To the extent that Shakespeare's plays are understood to be merely literary productions, they have no relevance to the important problems that agitate the lives of acting men.

But, when Shakespeare is read naïvely, because he shows most vividly and comprehensively the fate of tyrants, the character of good rulers, the relations of friends, and the duties of citizens, he can move the souls of his readers, and they recognize that they understand life better because they have read him; he hence becomes a constant guide and companion. He is turned to as the Bible was once turned to; one sees the world, enriched and embellished, through his eyes. It is this perspective that has been lost; and only when Shakespeare is taught as though he *said* something can he regain the influence over this generation which is so needed —needed for the sake of giving us some thoughtful views on the most important questions. The proper functions of criticism are, therefore, to recover Shakespeare's teaching and to be the agent of his ever-continuing education of the Anglo-Saxon world.

These essays are intended as first steps in the enterprise of making Shakespeare again the theme of philosophic reflection and a recognized source for the serious study of moral and political problems. The task is doubly difficult, for, not only must the subtle plays, difficult in themselves, be interpreted, but the authentic intellectual atmosphere in which they were written must be recovered. We no longer look at man, the state, or poetry as they were once looked at; and, without some clarity about the way Shakespeare saw them, all the careful study of the text will be of little avail. We would only see the things which we set out to find or which are within the range of our vision. The texts and their meaning are of course the only important things; the origins of Shakespeare's thought or its relation to its time are of relatively minor interest compared to the permanent significance of his meaning. It is this meaning that we must try to discover, but we must do so with full consciousness that it is no longer immediately accessible to us, owing to the passage of time and, more particularly, the vogue of new doctrines which have made our perspective other than that which Shakespeare counted on in his audience.

The authors of these essays are professors of political philosophy, which means that they are outside the field of Shakespearean criticism, given the current division of the academic disciplines. We respect the competence of our colleagues in the literature departments and are aware of the contributions of recent scholarship. But we contend that

Shakespeare is not the preserve of any single department in the modern university. He wrote before the university was divided as it is today, and the knowledge he presupposes cuts across these partly accidental lines. He presents us man generally, and it is not to be assumed that a department of literature possesses any privileged position for grasping his representations comprehensively. Consider a work like Rousseau's *Nouvelle Héloïse*—does it belong primarily to a philosophy department, a literature department, or a language department? Surely to all and to none; perhaps most of all to the educated amateur. We suggest that the case is the same with Shakespeare.

But, obviously, it is not solely on our amateur status that we base the claim that we have something to contribute. We believe that political philosophy is the proper beginning for the elaboration of the comprehensive framework within which the problems of the Shakespearean heroes can be viewed or, briefly, that Shakespeare was an eminently political author. Nothing puts us so far out of touch with contemporary beliefs and prejudices as this last claim, for both politics and philosophy have come to be understood as the opposites of poetry, and in some sense their study is supposed to make a man unfit to grasp the true sense of poetry.

The poetic, according to the modern argument, transcends the base public concerns of politics; the artist is closer to the antipolitical bohemian than to the political gentleman. As soon as one speaks of a political interpretation of poetry, one is suspected either of wanting to use poetry as an ideological weapon or of trying to import foreign doctrines—such as those of Marx or Freud—and making Shakespeare their unconscious precursor, all the while forgetting the plays themselves.

It is certainly true that the political teachings which underlie the modern state are prosaic—intentionally so. And, if the bourgeois, the man "motivated by fear of violent death," is the product of political life, the poetic must seek another field for its activity, since such a man, characterized only by the self-regarding passions, is not a proper subject of poetry. But political life was not always conceived in this way; it was classically thought to be the stage on which the broadest,

4

deepest, and noblest passions and virtues could be played, and the political man seemed to be the most interesting theme of poetry. It is at least plausible that, by taking our present notions of politics as eternal, we misinterpret the poetry of the past. In that case, we would be guilty of a grave historical error, an error which could be corrected by an open-minded study of the plays themselves.

Shakespeare devotes great care to establishing the political setting in almost all his plays, and his greatest heroes are rulers who exercise capacities which can only be exercised within civil society. To neglect this is simply to be blinded by the brilliance of one's own prejudices. As soon as one sees this, one cannot help asking what Shakespeare thought about a good regime and a good ruler. We contend that the man of political passions and education is in a better position to understand the plays than a purely private man. With the recognition of this fact, a new perspective is opened, not only on the plays but also on our notions of politics.

If politics is considered antithetical to poetry, philosophy is thought to be even more so, for poetry deals, it is said, with passions and sentiments, whereas philosophy bases itself on reason. The poet is the inspired creator, whereas the philosopher understands only what is. To this, again, it can only be responded that much of modern philosophy certainly seems to take no account of poetry, but it is not so clear that this is necessarily the case or that a poet cannot also be a thinker.

There is some question whether it would be possible for a man who had not thought a great deal about human nature to write a convincing drama. It is only an assumption that Shakespeare did not have a consistent and rational understanding of man which he illustrated in his plays; only a final and complete interpretation of them all could demonstrate that this is so. On the face of it, the man who could write *Macbeth* so convincingly that a Lincoln believed it to be the perfect illustration of the problems of tyranny and murder must have known about politics; otherwise, however charming its language, the play would not have attracted a man who admittedly did know. The contemporary antagonism between philosophy and poetry is a child of our age; it might serve most profitably to remind us of another kind of philosophy, one which could talk sensibly about human things, and of another kind of poetry, one which could unite the charm of the passions with the rigor of the intellect.

I I

Shakespeare wrote at a time when common sense still taught that the function of the poet was to produce pleasure and that the function of the great poet was to teach what is truly beautiful by means of pleasure. Common sense was supported by a long tradition which had a new burst of vitality in the Renaissance. Socrates had said that Homer was the teacher of the Greeks, and he meant by that that those who ruled Greece had their notions of what kind of men they would like to be set for them by the Homeric epics. Achilles was the authentic hero, and his glory was that against which all later heroes up to Alexander competed. A man who knew Homer was a Greek. If we follow Herodotus, Homer, along with Hesiod, also invented the gods in the forms in which they were worshiped by later generations. He was the true founder of his people, for he gave them what made them distinctive, invented that soul for which they are remembered. Such are the ambitions of the great poet. Goethe understood this:

> A great dramatic poet, if he is at the same time productive and is actuated by a strong noble purpose which pervades all his works, may succeed in making the soul of his plays become the soul of the people. I should think that this was well worth the trouble. From Corneille proceeded an influence capable of forming heroes. This was something for Napoleon, who had need of a heroic people, on which account he said of Corneille that, if he were still living, he would make a prince of him. A dramatic poet who knows his vocation should therefore work incessantly at its higher development in order that his influence on the people may be noble and beneficial.[1]

As Napoleon knew, it is *only* a poet who can give a people such inspiration.

Poetry is the most powerful form of rhetoric, a form which goes beyond ordinary rhetoric in that it shapes the men on whom the statesman's rhetoric can work. The philosopher

6

cannot move nations; he speaks only to a few. The poet can take the philosopher's understanding and translate it into images which touch the deepest passions and cause men to know without knowing that they know. Aristotle's description of heroic virtue means nothing to men in general, but Homer's incarnation of that virtue in the Greeks and Trojans is unforgettable. This desire to depict the truth about man and to make other men fulfill that truth is what raises poetry to its greatest heights in the epic and the drama. Poetry takes on its significance, in both its content and its uses, from the political nobility of the poet. Poetry is not autonomous; its life is infused by its attachment to the same objects which motivate the best of acting men.

The poet's task is a double one—to understand the things he wishes to represent and to understand the audience to which he speaks. He must know about the truly permanent human problems; otherwise his works will be slight and passing. There must be parallelism between what he speaks of and the most vital concerns of his audience; without that, his works will be mere tributes to the virtuosity of his techniques. In the great work, one is unaware of the technique and even of the artist; one is only conscious that the means are perfectly appropriate to the ends. The beauty of the words is but a reflection of the beauty of the thing; the poet is immersed in the thing, which is the only source of true beauty. And he must know what to touch in his audience. A photograph of a man does not usually convey the character of a man; that is grasped in certain traits which may rarely be seen. The painter can abstract all that is not essential to that impression, and he knows how the eye of the viewer will see the man. Certain illusions are often necessary to see the man as he really is; the sense of reality is transmitted in a medium of unreality. So the poet, too, must know how to play on his audience, how to transform its vision while taking it for what it is. That audience is a complex animal made up of many levels. To each he must speak, appealing to the simple souls as well as to the subtle. Thus, his poem is complex and has many levels, just as does the audience; it is designed first for the conventional order composed of aristocracy and commoners, but more profoundly for the natural order composed of those who understand and those who do not. The poet knows the characters of men from both looking at them and speaking to them. That is why the intelligent man takes him seriously; he has a kind of experience with men that the practitioner of no other art or science possesses.

The poet is an imitator of nature; he reproduces what he sees in the world, and it is only his preoccupation with that world which renders him a poet. He is not a creator, for that would mean that he makes something from nothing; were he to look only within himself, he would find a void—a void destined by nature itself to be filled with knowledge of the essential articulations of things. What distinguishes a good poet from a bad one is whether he has seen things as they are and learned to distinguish the superficial from the profound. In particular, poetry imitates man, and this means—according to the classical tradition which I am elaborating—his virtues and his vices. A man is most what he is as a result of what he does; a man is known, not simply by his existence, but by the character of his actions—liberal or greedy, courageous or cowardly, frank or sly, moderate or profligate. Since these qualities produce happiness or misery, they are of enduring interest to human beings. Hence they are the specific subject matter of poetry. Passions, feelings, and the whole realm of the psychological are secondary. This is because feelings are properly related to certain kinds of action and to the virtues which control such action; they are formless when considered by themselves. Jealousy and ambition have to do with love and politics and gain their particular qualities from the particular objects to which they are directed and the particular men who feel them; therefore, the primary concern of the poet is with the various kinds of human action. The plot, the story of a series of actions which leads to prosperity or misfortune, is the soul of the play and that which guides all else, including the portrayal of psychological affections.

Human virtues and vices can be said to be defined primarily in political terms. Civil society and its laws define what is good and bad, and its education forms the citizens. The character of life is decisively influenced by the character of the regime under which a man lives, and it is the regime that encourages or discourages the growth within it of the various human types. Any change in a way of life presupposes a

8

change in the political, and it is by means of the political that the change must be effected. It is in their living together that men develop their human potential, and it is the political regime which determines the goals and the arrangement of the life in common. Moreover, it is in ruling and being ruled, in the decisions concerning war and peace, that men exercise their highest capacities. There may be situations in which men have no chance to be rulers, but, to the degree to which they are excluded from political life, they are less fully developed and satisfied. In political life, not only are the ordinary virtues projected on a larger screen, but totally new capacities are brought into play. The political provides the framework within which all that is human can develop itself; it attracts the most interesting passions and the most interesting men. Hence, the dramatist who wishes to represent man most perfectly will usually choose political heroes. Because of his artistic freedom, he can paint his figures more characteristically, less encumbered by fortuitous traits, than can a historian.

What is essentially human is revealed in the extreme, and we understand ourselves better through what we might be. In a way, the spectators live more truly when they are watching a Shakespearean play than in their daily lives, which are so much determined by the accidents of time and place. There could be a theater dealing totally with the private life, the cares of providing for a living and raising a family. But men who never got beyond that life would be cut off from their fullest human development, and a theater which acquiesced in that view of human life would be only a tool in increasing the enslavement to it.

This is a popular account of the traditional view of the drama, that which was current in Shakespeare's time; it is more likely that he shared it than that he held anything like the modern view. It is not necessary to argue that he himself had reflected on it; it was in the air, and he would come naturally to think about things in these terms. But, in fact, it seems clear on the basis of the evidence provided by the histories that Shakespeare did, indeed, elaborate his intentions and consciously wanted his works to convey his political wisdom. In these plays, he tried to develop a sensible view of what the English regime is and how it should be accepted and revered by succeeding generations of Englishmen. He was successful in this attempt, for the English do understand their history and what it represents much as he depicted it. Here his intention was clearly political, and his understanding of what is both beautiful and exciting to his audience is based primarily on the concerns of civil society. Is it plausible to say that this was just a series of good stories? They are, indeed, good stories, but they are that precisely because of the kind of interest they evoke. Can one reasonably say that he dashed off the historical plays because he needed money or that he was ignorant of the essential facts of English history because he had never studied? This would be as much as to say that Jefferson, with no consideration of political principle, wrote the Declaration of Independence because he wanted to be well known and that its success is due to its being an excellent Fourth of July oration.

What is so manifestly true of the histories could well be true of the tragedies and comedies, too. Shakespeare's humanity was not limited to England or to making Englishmen good citizens of England. There is a whole series of fundamental human problems, and I suggest that Shakespeare intended to depict all of them and that the man who, *per impossibile*, could understand all the plays individually would see the consequences of all the possible important choices of ways of life and understand fully the qualities of the various kinds of good soul. But that takes me beyond the scope of this introduction; I allude to it only to indicate the range of Shakespeare's genius. For the moment, it is sufficient to suggest the possibility that, for the other plays, just as for the histories, Shakespeare may have seen politics as, at the least, very important, that he had a pedagogic intention, and that his learning was sufficient to make him aware of the fundamental alternatives, theoretical and practical.

If this is so, political philosophy would be essential to our interpretation of his works. However wrong Shakespeare may have been about the real nature of poetry as discovered by modern criticism, in understanding him we would have to use his framework instead of trying to squeeze him into our new categories. Every rule of objectivity requires that an author first be understood as he understood himself; without that, the work is nothing but what we make of it. The role of political philosophy in Shakespearean criticism would be to give a discursive account of the goals of the passions depicted in the plays. When Sextus Pompeius is given the choice of murdering his guests and becoming emperor of the universe or remaining within the pale of decency and being done away with himself, we are confronted with a classic problem of political morality, one that is presented with detail and precision in *Antony and Cleopatra*. We must recognize it as such, and we must further have some knowledge of the kinds of men who desire to rule and of what this desire does to them. It is only in philosophic discussion that we find a development of these problems, and from that we can help to clarify the problems of which Shakespeare gives us models. In our day, we are particularly in need of the history of political philosophy, for we are not immediately aware of the various possible understandings of the political and moral phenomena and must seek those which most adequately explain what Shakespeare presents to us.

Shakespeare has set his plays in many nations and at various times in history. This is a good beginning for the investigation of his teaching, for various nations encourage various virtues in men; one cannot find every kind of man in any particular time and place. Just the difference between paganism and Christianity has an important effect on the kinds of preoccupations men have. To present the various possibilities, the typical men have to be in an environment in which they can flourish. The dates and places of Shakespeare's plays were chosen with a view to revealing the specific interests of the heroes. It was only in Venice that Othello and Shylock could act out their potentials; they were foreigners, and only Venice provided them freedom and a place in the city. Only in Rome could one see the course of political ambition free of other goals which mitigate it. It would be a worthwhile project to spend a lifetime studying the settings of the plays in relation to the plots, trying to see what are the typical problems of what time and what nation. All this would be with a view to distinguishing what Shakespeare thought the best kinds of men and what advantages and disadvantages go with what ways of life. We are in need of generations of criticism—naïve criticism which asks the kinds of questions of Shakespeare that Glaucon and Adeimantus once posed to Socrates. How should we live? Is it best to be a ruler or a poet? Can one kill a king? Should one's parents be disobeyed for the sake of love? And so on endlessly.

Schiller pointed out that modern times are characterized by abstract science on the one hand and unrefined passions on the other and that the two have no relation. A free man and a good citizen must have a natural harmony between his passions and his knowledge; this is what is meant by a man of taste, and it is he whom we today seem unable to form. We are aware that a political science which does not grasp the moral phenomena is crude and that an art uninspired by the passion for justice is trivial. Shakespeare wrote before the separation of these things; we sense that he has both intellectual clarity and vigorous passions and that the two do not undermine each other in him. If we live with him a while, perhaps we can recapture the fullness of life and rediscover the way to its lost unity.

NOTES

1 Johann Peter Eckermann, *Conversations with Goethe*, April 1, 1827.

2

＋＊＋◎＋＊＋◎＋＊＋◎＋＊＋◎＋＊＋◎＋＊＋◎＋＊＋◎＋＊＋◎＋＊＋◎＋＊＋◎＋＊

On Christian and Jew

❧ *THE MERCHANT OF VENICE* * ❧

VENICE IS a beautiful city, full of color and variety. To this day it represents the exotic and the exciting to the minds of those who know it—a port with all the freedom that the proximity to the sea seems to encourage and with the presence of diverse kinds of men from diverse nations, races, and religions brought by the hope of adventure or gain to its shores. The prosperous merchants of Venice lavishly adorned it in a romantic taste, combining the styles of East and West, between which it was the link. Add to this the sun of Italy and the attractiveness of its people and you have that city which remains the setting of dreams of pleasure and happiness.

Shakespeare, in his two Venetian plays, *Othello* and *The Merchant of Venice* admirably captures the atmosphere of

* This article is based on a lecture given at the Hillel Foundation of the University of Chicago in January, 1960. I wish to dedicate it to the memory of Rabbi Maurice B. Pekarsky, the director of that organization for seventeen years. He was a wise and good man who inspired men of many faiths with respect for Judaism; he appealed on the highest grounds to both heart and mind.

Venice. It is not surprising that he chose this locale in which to present his most exotic heroes; Othello and Shylock are the figures who are the most foreign to the context in which they move and to the audience for which they were intended. In a sense, it is Shakespeare's achievement in the two plays to have made these two men—who would normally have been mere objects of hatred and contempt—into human beings who are unforgettable for their strength of soul. For the first time in European literature, there was a powerful characterization of men so different; Shakespeare, while proving his own breadth of sympathy, made an impression on his audiences which could not be eradicated. Whether they liked these men or not, the spectators now knew they were men and not things on which they could with impunity exercise their vilest passions. Venice offered the perfect setting for the actions of Shylock and Othello because it was the place where the various sorts of men could freely mingle, and it was known the world over as the most tolerant city of its time. In this city, those men who, it was generally thought, could never share a common way of life seemed to live together in harmony.

Shakespeare, however, does not depict Venice with the bright colors which one would expect, given its beauty and its promise. When one thinks of Othello or Shylock, one can only remember their somber fates. In both cases, I believe, their unhappy destinies were in some measure a result of their foreignness, or, in other words, Venice did not fulfill for them its promise of being a society in which men could live as men, not as whites and blacks, Christians and Jews, Venetians and foreigners. To understand why Shakespeare has thus presented Venice, we must for a moment consider what it meant to enlightened men in the sixteenth and seventeenth centuries.

I

Venice was a republic—one of the few successful examples of such a political organization in its time. It had for several hundred years guarded its independence. It had an orderly form of government in which a large proportion of the citizens could take active part. It was prosperous and had even become powerful enough, in spite of its size, to cherish some imperial ambitions. During the Renaissance, there was a revival of the republican spirit among thoughtful men; it was thought that the proper practice of political life had deteriorated since the fall of the Roman Republic. For whatever reasons, the political—the condition of human dignity—had become indifferent to men, and they lived under monarchs. The independence and pride that are a result of self-government had vanished; the political virtues praised by the ancients had no opportunity for exercise and withered away. One can find this point of view developed most completely in Machiavelli, but it was shared by many eminent thinkers. Nonetheless, public-spirited men also looked for examples of the possibility of republics in modern times, and Venice was the most fitting one. From the end of the sixteenth century to the middle of the seventeenth, Venice was constantly admired and written about as the model of a good political order in modernity. It preceded Amsterdam as the model and —to name only two of its most illustrious advocates—Harrington and Spinoza drew liberally on it in the elaborations of their teachings. It was, indeed, a modern state and hence different from Rome in many crucial respects. It is in these respects that it was of most interest to modern theorists, because it seemed to provide an answer to their central problems.

Along with the taste for republicanism came a certain depreciation of the Biblical religions, partly because their other-worldliness seemed to be the source of the disinterest in the political and partly because they were at the root of the religious fanaticism which issued in such occurrences as the Religious Wars and the Inquisition. These religious attachments, it was believed, led men away from their political interests and divided them on the basis of opinions. Modern republicanism had to overcome the religious question, to attach men to the here and now rather than to the hereafter. The state had to become tolerant to be able to embrace in a stable order men of widely differing beliefs. This was a problem not directly addressed by ancient political thought, and its resolution is the most characteristic aspect of later political thought. It was believed that only by directing men's interest to something which could subordinate their religious attachments would it be possible to establish a way of life in which religious doctrines and their intransigence would not play the leading part. It was not thought possible to educate men to a tolerant view or to overcome the power of the established religions by refuting them; the only way was to substitute for the interest and concern of men's passions another object as powerfully attractive as religion.

Such an object was to be found in the jealous desire for gain. The commercial spirit causes men to moderate their fanaticism; men for whom money is the most important thing are unlikely to go off on Crusades. Venice was above all a commercial city and had indeed succeeded in bringing together in one place more types of men than any other city.[1] The condition of Shylock's living in Venice was its need of venture capital for its enterprises. The laws which would not be respected for themselves were obeyed because they were the foundation of the city's prosperity. As the Merchant himself says:

> The Duke cannot deny the course of law:
> For the commoditie that strangers have
> With us in Venice, if it be denied,
> Will much impeach the justice of the state
> Since that the trade and profit of the city
> Consisteth of all nations.[2]

The Jews in Venice were well off and enjoyed the full protection of the law in the fifteenth and sixteenth centuries; the Venice Jewish community was relatively privileged among the Jewish communities in the Diaspora. Shylock's claim against Antonio rests entirely on that law, and he is perfectly aware of its commercial roots. Venice was a model city for the new political thought; it was tolerant, bourgeois, and republican. This solution to the political problem is the one which became dominant in the West and is only too familiar to us.

It behooves us, therefore, to examine Shakespeare's view of that city which contained the germ of what is today generally accepted. He did in that city, as I have said, present his view of the relations among men who are foreign to one another. This is the link between the two Venetian plays. He understood the hopes based on the Venetian experiment, and, as the fates of his heroes show, he was pessimistic about the possibilities of its success. This is not to say that he did not approve of what Venice stood for; but he tried to understand the human consequences of the legal arrangements, and he found that friendship between such unlike personages is very difficult, if not impossible. Laws are not sufficient; they must be accompanied by good dispositions on the parts of those who live under them. Shakespeare presents the depths of souls as no man has ever done, and through his divine insight we can catch sight of the difficulties which stand in the way of human brotherhood—difficulties which are real and cannot be done away with by pious moralizing.

I I

Shylock and Antonio are Jew and Christian, and they are at war as a result of their difference in faith. It is not that they misunderstand each other because of a long history of prejudice and that enlightenment could correct their hostility; rather, their real views of the world, their understanding of what is most important in life, are so opposed that they could never agree. When confronted with each other in the same place in relation to the same people, they must necessarily quarrel. Their difference as to whom and on what terms one should lend money is the most external sign of this root-and-branch opposition. To do away with their hostility, the beliefs of each would have to be done away with—those beliefs which go from the very depths to the heights of their souls. In other words, their being would have to be changed, for men are constituted most essentially by their understanding of the most important things. The law of Venice can force them to a temporary truce, but in any crucial instance the conflict will re-emerge, and each will try to destroy the spirit of the law; for each has a different way of life which, if it were universalized within the city, would destroy that of the other. They have no common ground.

Antonio and Shylock are, however, not merely individuals who differ; Shakespeare, rightly or wrongly, has presented them as types, representatives of Judaism and Christianity. Each acts according to the principles of his faith. They do not differ because they are men who have idiosyncrasies, but because their principles are opposed; those principles are not their own, but are derived from their respective religions. Of course, we do not see them in the purity of their worship; they act in the corrupt world of private and political life. But we do see the extension of their principles in that world. Antonio and Shylock are each depicted as models of their heritage; each is even a parody of a remarkable Biblical figure, not as those figures were but as they might be in the context of Venice. Shakespeare views them from outside without considering the truth of either.[3]

Shylock holds that respect for and obedience to the *law* is the condition for leading a decent life. Throughout the play, law is his only appeal and his only claim. Righteousness is hence the criterion for goodness; if a man obeys the law to its letter throughout his life, he will prosper and do what is human. No other consideration need trouble him. Justice is lawfulness; Shylock is a son of Moses. Along with this goes a certain positive temper; Shylock lives very much in this world. Money is a solid bastion of comfortable existence, not for the sake of pleasure or refinement, but for that of family and home. The beggar is contemptible and was probably not righteous. This earth is where man lives, and justice and injustice reap the fruits of reward and punishment on it. Decent sobriety is the rule of life, each man living for himself according to the rule. A certain toughness and lack of far-ranging sympathies characterize him.[4]

Moreover, shrewdness concerning the things about which the law does not speak is perfectly legitimate and even desirable. To live well on this earth, one must have some amount of substance, without which life is miserable; given the nature of men, one is likely to lose what properly belongs to one, if one is not careful. Shylock's model is Jacob, who had to deceive his father to attain his succession and who used tricks to get a fair wage from Laban.[5] So he is a moneylender; he does not cheat men—he only takes advantage of their need. If a man wants money for his business or his pleasures, he can make use of what Shylock possesses.

Shylock does not care for the man or his interests, but through them he can profit himself. What he does is neither noble nor generous, but it is not unjust. Why should he concern himself with Bassanio's prodigality or his hopes to make a good match for himself? Would it not be folly to waste one's sympathy and one's substance on the vices of others? Shylock lives privately in his "sober home" with his daughter, and this way of life is protected by his shrewdness and the money which he earned with it.

Antonio, on the contrary, bases his whole life on generosity and love for his fellow man. For him, the law, in its intransigence and its indifference to persons, is an inadequate guide for life. Not that one should ignore the law, but it is only a minimum condition. Equity and charity are more important virtues than righteousness. Antonio has money; it is, however, not for his own enjoyment, but rather for his friends. He lends his money but not for profit. Life on this earth is but a frail thing and only gains whatever allure it has in seeing others made happy. Antonio is sad, and life does not mean much to him. Life is but a stage, and our actions take on meaning only in a larger context. Antonio is perfectly willing to die for his friend to prove how much he loves him. Calm calculation is beyond him. He makes promises he cannot keep, and his hopes are based on ships that are yet to come in. The restraint and the coldness of the Jew are not his; his sympathies go out to all men, and he cares much for their affection. He is full of sentimentality. He has no family, and we hear nothing of his home; he is a bachelor.[6]

Antonio and Shylock are not made to understand each other. When Shylock sees Antonio approaching, he says, "How like a fawning publican he looks," echoing the sentiments of the Pharisee in the Gospel who prides himself on his own righteousness and despises the publican's abasement before the Lord.[7] Antonio in his turn has, in imitation of Jesus, driven the moneylenders from the Rialto. He has spit on Shylock, for his sympathy cannot extend to a man who denies the fundamental principle of charity.[8] That is the limit case. Neither can regard the other as a human being in any significant sense because in all that is human they differ. It is very well to tell them to live together, but in any confrontation of the two they are bound to quarrel. What is prudence for one is robbery for the other; what is kindness for one is mawkish sentimentality to the other. There is no middle ground, since they see the same objects as different things; common sense cannot mediate between them. If there is to be harmony, one must give in to the other; pride, at least, if not conviction, precludes this. But the two men need each other; they are linked by money. Antonio must borrow from Shylock. They have a contract, but one that is not bound by good faith.

In this not-very-funny comedy, the most amusing figure is the clown, Launcelot Gobbo. He is so amusing largely because he represents the ridiculousness of the man who tries to live in the worlds of Antonio and Shylock at the same time; everything is so different that he is like someone who wants to stand on his head and his feet at the same time. He works for the Jew, but his conscience tells him that the Jew is the Devil; so he wants to leave the Jew, but his conscience tells him that he must do his duty. His conscience, that great instrument of moral guidance, tells him that he must go and stay at the same time. Launcelot is utterly confused. Ultimately, he follows the only thing he knows surely, his stomach. Shylock's parsimony has left him hungry; also, Bassanio gives pretty uniforms, a thing unthinkable in the home of the austere Jew. There seem to be no rules of moral conduct which can govern the relationship between men so diverse. Launcelot draws out the paradox of the situation when he discusses Jessica's conversion with her. She can, he says, only be saved if her father were not her father; but, if her sin of being the Jew's daughter is removed, she will inherit the sin of her mother's adultery. She is damned if she does and damned if she doesn't. Besides, Launcelot, on his gastro-economic grounds, is against conversion because it will make the price of pork go up.[9]

Shylock states his principle for relating to the Christian community in which he lives as follows: "I will buy with you, sell with you, talke with you, walke with you, and so following: but I will not eate with you, drinke with you, nor pray with you."[10] What is most important to him he cannot share with his neighbors. When men do not agree about what is most important, they can hardly be said to constitute a community. *Othello* is about a man who tried to assimilate and failed. In *The Merchant of Venice,* we see the soul of a man who refused to assimilate. He is consequently distrusted and hated. He reciprocates, and his soul is poisoned.

I I I

Shylock makes one compromise with his principle. He goes to dinner at Bassanio's. Punishment is swift and harsh. During the dinner, he loses his daughter plus a considerable sum of money. Everything that he has held most dear is gone; he becomes a monster intent only on revenge. It is no longer principle which guides him, for he has compromised his principle by disobeying the law. He can only think that Antonio arranged the dreadful deed, although Antonio apparently knew nothing of it.[11] Shylock recognizes that no one cares for him, that his sorrows are the joys of others. No humiliation could be more complete; as a man with dignity, he can only make others suffer for what he suffers. Others have counted him out of the pale of humanity, and he will show them that they were right in doing so. Formerly, he was bitter, but he had his little life in which he could practice his faith and enjoy his home. Now this is all gone. He has a certain grandeur in the depth of his rage, but he has become terrible. The strong impression he makes is based only on that which is negative in him. How could he forgive when he would only be despised for his forgiveness? If he cannot be loved, he can at least gain the respect of fear. But now his life is carried on only in response to the Christians whom he hates; it has no solid content of its own. In this portrayal, Shakespeare to some extent gives justification to the Christian reproach that the Jews had lost the one most important thing and carried on only the empty forms of their law.

Shylock is not a comic figure. There is no scene in the play in which he is meant to be laughed at in person. He does appear comic in the eyes of some of the Christian actors, but this only proves that Shakespeare did not agree with them and is as much of a commentary on them as on Shylock. He is most comic to Salerino and Solanio, who burlesque his screaming after his ducats, his daughter and his ducats.[12] Shylock is reproached, as were the Jews in general, for materialism, a materialism which made it impossible to make proper distinctions between things. This is borne out by Shylock's conduct, but in no ignoble way. For him, as we have said, life is an earthly thing, and his money is connected intrinsically with his existence. His affection for his daughter is based on the fact that she is his flesh and blood.[13] The so-called spiritual ties do not exist for him; everything he has belongs to him in the same intimate way that his body belongs to him. There is no distinction between spirit and matter; the relation of souls alone without the other bonds is impossible; therefore, a universal humanity is excluded. Kinship is the source of love; hence, his real loves are his family and his "sacred nation."

When Shylock talks to Tubal about his daughter and his money, he does indeed express the sentiments attributed to him by his ridiculers, but they appear very differently to us.[14] He would like to see his daughter dead with the jewels in her ear. We are shocked by the distortion of the sentiment, but we also see that his daughter is more a part of him than his money, that this is an expression of the depth of his loss. Jessica does not belong to him any more; all he can count on now is his money. She has broken the law and defied him. She is no more, and he must forget her, for she existed as a human for him only as long as she was faithful. It is a hard code, but the passion and discipline that are required to obey it are a measure of what it means to Shylock. As Jessica was hated with intensity when she left the fold, so she would have been loved if she had remained within it. Shylock's daughter is dead to him, but part of him has also died. The feeling of which Shylock is capable is seen in the admirable response he makes when he hears that Jessica has bartered for a monkey the turquoise he gave his wife. "I would not have given it for a wilderness of monkies." [15] This is the expression of a man practiced to a parsimony of sentiment, but whose sentiments for that reason are deep and unutterable. It differs from the effusiveness of Antonio's expressions of love, but is it not equal?

The most quoted speech in *The Merchant of Venice* is the one which best of all shows the plight of Shylock:

I am a Jew: Hath not a Jew eyes? Hath not a Jew hands, organs, dementions, sences, affections, passions, fed with the same foode, hurt with the same weapons, subject to the same diseases, healed by the same meanes, warmed and cooled by the same Winter and Sommer as a Christian is: if you pricke us doe we not bleede? If you tickle us, doe we not laugh? if you poison us doe we not die? and if you wrong us shall we not revenge? if we are like you in the rest, we will resemble you in that.[16]

Shylock justifies himself by an appeal to the universality of humanity. Behind this harsh but touching complaint is a plea for the exercise of the Golden Rule. Men can only be men together when they mutually recognize their sameness; otherwise they are like beings of different species to each other, and their only similarity is in their revenge. But, sadly, if one looks at the list of similar characteristics on which Shylock bases his claim to equality with his Christian tormentors, one sees that it includes only things which belong to the body; what he finds in common between Christian and Jew is essentially what all animals have in common. The only spiritual element in the list is revenge.[17] Like Antiphon the sophist, Shylock asserts that the brotherhood of man can only come into being on the basis of the lowest common denominator, and that common denominator is very low indeed. It is the body; all the higher parts of the soul must be abstracted from, because they express men's opinions and beliefs about what is good and bad, virtue and vice. These, men do not share; these beliefs make men enemies. Shylock appeals to a humanity which all men can recognize, but in so doing he must discount what all noble men would regard as the most important.

Shylock stands for Judaism, and his life has gained its sense from that fact, not from the fact that he eats, drinks, and feels; Christianity has played a similar role in the lives of his opponents. They would have to transform their beings in order to become unified. The choice seems to be a hostile diversity on a high level or a common humanity on the level of the beasts—a common humanity grounded on an indifference to the opinion about the nature of the good. The four Jewish names in *The Merchant of Venice* seem to be drawn from two successive chapters, 10 and 11, of Genesis. Chapter 11 has as its theme the Tower of Babel; perhaps this is part of Shakespeare's meaning. "Let us go down and there confound their language, that they may not understand one another's speech." Men's separateness is an act of divine providence.[18]

IV

Whether or not Shylock originally intended to exact the pound of flesh if possible, after the loss of Jessica his whole hope was to be able to gain revenge within the limits of the law. The drama of Shylock and Antonio would have come to a disastrous end if it had not been for Portia. The contrast between Portia and the other two major figures is sharp, and the difference in atmosphere between Belmont and Venice is striking. Portia brings with her a love of gaiety, satisfaction, subtlety, and, above all, common sense that is entirely lacking in Venice. While scenes of hate are being unfolded in Venice, at Belmont Portia presides over a feast of love—love, not in the sense of Antonio's spiritual love for Bassanio, but of the erotic love between man and woman. Portia is the master of this world of Belmont, and her own satisfaction is the highest law of the land. She has no doctrines, and she is willing to appear to be anything to achieve her ends. She rules, and rules for her own good, while always keeping up the appearances of propriety and justice. Belmont is beautiful, and there we enter the realm of the senses. It is pagan; everyone there speaks in the terms of classical antiquity. Religion is only used there, and there is even a temple for the Moor. The themes of conversation and the ideas current in Belmont have an ancient source. Portia has the tastes of a Roman and is compared to one whose name she shares.[19]

Belmont, too, is a cosmopolitan place, but the attraction there is not money but love. Men from all over the world come to woo the fair Portia, and she is able to see and evaluate what the wide world has to offer. She is no cloistered little girl. She presents a typology of national characteristics in going over the list of her suitors—the horse-loving Neapolitan, the severe Pole, the drinking German, and so forth. She judges them each in relation to the commodity of a pleasant shared existence. Her candor when she is alone with her servant is shocking to some and exasperating to others, but it can also appear to be the clear vision of one who is liberated and has spurned the unhappy depths of tragedy. Portia rejoices in the beauties of the surface, and certainly no one can assert that her hedonism leads to vulgarity. She chooses for her husband a fellow countryman after having seen all that is exotic and strange. She is the opposite of the shy, untutored Desdemona. She opts for the familiar, not only because it is the familiar, but also because it represents most adequately what is agreeable and appropriate to her; Bassanio is a sort of mean in relation to the other suitors, just as is his nation speaking geographically.

The test of the three caskets shows the principles implied in Portia's choice as well as it prefigures the technique she will use in the trial. Portia is apparently not the mistress of her fate; she is ruled by the will of her father, who has decreed that the man who is to win her must first pass a seemingly foolish test of character. Portia professes dissatisfaction with this arrangement, but, as a good daughter, she intends to abide by the restriction. She does not, like Desdemona or Jessica, defy conventions to gain the object of her wishes; she has a great respect for the forms, if not the substance, of the conventional. The test is, moreover, not entirely disagreeable, because its conditions drive off many an undesirable suitor who might otherwise be importunate. She uses her traditional duty to satisfy her desires, but, as becomes clear, does not become its victim.

The first suitor who risks the choice is a Moor, who begins his wooing with the request: "Mislike me not for my complexion." He is in certain respects like Othello, but rendered comic in the atmosphere created by Portia. He is a great warrior and a passionate lover, full of noble words. This hasty man of the South chooses the golden casket because of its appearance. He is a slave of his senses. Portia, who has treated him with elaborate politeness, dismisses him from her thoughts with, "Let all of his complexion choose me so." She is no Desdemona who "saw Othello's visage in his mind." [20] She makes no effort to transform her immediate sensual impressions. She knows the sort of man who would be to her taste.

As the Moor was immediate, sensual, and passionate, Aragon is the cool, reflected gentleman of the North. He is a pious moralizer, full of the most correct commonplaces. He chooses the moderate silver, and the basis of his judgment is the text. He chooses to have his just desert, but is angry when his deserving turns out to be less than what he conceives.[21] Aragon is a fool who thinks that the accents of virtue constitute its essence. Portia sees in him only a bore. The Moor chose by images; Aragon, by texts. Neither is right. Portia seeks a man who can combine feeling and thought in a natural grace of sentiment. The South is barbaric; the North, cold and sententious. True civilization implies a mixture of developed understanding and reflection with a full capacity to perceive; one must both see things as they are and react to them appropriately. Texts and images must go together as a natural unity.

Portia wants Bassanio. She is aware that he is not a hero, that he is not her equal. She knows his weaknesses and even the fact that he hopes to recoup his fortunes by marriage. But she also sees that he is a nice man, a man of refined sentiments, and a true gentleman. He does not sermonize, and he is balanced and graceful in his judgments. He is neither primitive nor overcivilized. He has no eminent virtues, but he pretends to none, and he has no marked vices. He is a mean; he is both handsome and cultivated. Bassanio is also no fanatic. He is the only one of the Venetians who does not instinctively hate Shylock. He always treats him like a man, indifferent to the doctrines which separate them. He is surprised and shocked at Shylock's conduct; he does not expect it, and even encourage it, as does Antonio. Bassanio is humane and simple. Like Portia, he approaches the world with no preconceptions, but lets impression and taste guide him; but his is an educated taste. He loves Portia, and Portia wants him. So she cheats and lets Bassanio know how to choose by the song she sings. It depreciates the senses, and its meaning is clear. Moreover, the first rhyme is "bred" with "head," which also rhyme with "lead." Bassanio's own reflections are very just and show a capacity to put text and image together, but he is assured of choosing aright by the song. Portia does this delicately; but, by using the convention which seems to limit her, she becomes the master of her fate. She breaks her faith, but in such a way that the appearances are saved, thus preserving the principle without being a victim of the principle. The law is only a means to an end with her.[22]

V

Portia goes off to Venice to save Antonio, not out of any principle of universal humanity, but because he is her husband's friend, and Bassanio is involved in the responsibility for his plight. She leaves on the pious pretext of going to a nunnery to prepare herself for marriage and takes on a new appearance, that of a boy.[23] She becomes a representative of the law and interjects herself as such between the warring Jew and Christian. The situation between them has become intolerable; only senseless bestiality can be the consequence. Shylock lives only for revenge; the law supports him. He desires the flesh of Antonio, although it can profit him in no way. There is no compromise possible.[24] Shylock knows that he is hated and that he can never have respect from the others. He has no private life to which he can retreat with dignity; that is all gone. He would seem weak or cowardly if he gave in. Antonio, on the other hand, is not entirely averse to martyrdom. It fits well with his general melancholy, and he can prove his great love by dying for Bassanio. He can make an ever-living memorial for himself in the guilt of his friend, whom he expects to write an epitaph for him.[25] Only by altering the law can this absurd situation, which law never intended, be avoided. But the essence of the law is its fixity. Only a Portia, indifferent to the law but aware of its power, can manipulate it.[26]

Portia understands Shylock's intention quickly; she knows that law is what counts for him. So she presents herself at the beginning as the severest interpreter of the law, which wins Shylock's confidence. First, in a most direct and frank way, she tries to settle the case without chicanery. Shylock must be merciful. She does not appeal directly to his simple humanity; she knows that Shylock is a Jew and that she must begin from there. She tries to suggest a common ground on which Jew and Christian can meet, and not the low one of animal nature. She tries to show that both have the Scripture in common, that they pray to the same god with the same prayer, the Lord's Prayer. Christian and Jew do share on a high level, and neither need step out of his faith to experience the unity. And the present case is covered by the community of faith. "Forgive us our debts as we forgive our debtors." Equity and mercy stand above the law.[27] But this noble attempt does not succeed, at least with Shylock. The interpretation of the meaning of the same Scripture differs too much between the two. The law, and only the law, is still the highest for Shylock.

Portia tries a second mode of reconciliation through the mean motive of profit. This, too, fails, and now Portia starts using her wiles. First she gains Shylock's acceptance of her adjudication by the appearance of strict interpretation of the law. He puts himself completely into her hands—"a Daniel, come to judge me." Then, by a series of steps which we need not recount, she turns the tables on Shylock and deprives him of his revenge, his fortune, and his Judaism. Her means are contrary to all good legal proceeding. Portia, in demanding that the flesh be cut to the exact weight and that no drop of blood be spilled, makes it impossible to achieve ends that have been agreed to be legitimate. With particular reference to the blood, she asks for a miracle: flesh must have the qualities of nonflesh. That would be as great a miracle as the reverse. Shylock's faith in the righteousness of his cause apparently does not go so far as to count on divine intervention. The age of miracles is past.

Portia has maintained the appearance of the law, and the case is settled. Shylock suffers terribly; with the loss of his revenge, he has lost everything. Someone had to suffer in this terrible affair, and Shylock was the one who in justice should do so. He insisted on the inhuman. The war of Shylock and Antonio could not go on, and Portia decides in favor of Antonio. Venice is a Christian city, and Antonio her husband's friend. If the cancer of civil discord must be rooted out, then Shylock is the one to go.

Conversion is no solution.[28] We can all see that Shylock is now a dead man. Justice has not been done to him in any complete sense. Shakespeare wishes to leave a doleful impression of the impossibility of the harmonious resolution of such problems. He does this with the unforgettable picture of

Shylock's grandeur and misery. But Shylock is not a nice man.

It has been remarked that Shylock's reduction to nothingness is too quick and too improbable. Is it plausible that Shylock, who has evinced such pride, would give in to Portia in such a cowardly way? This would make him like those Jews of the earlier literature who were only devices of plot. I believe that those who make this objection have missed the genius of the trial scene. It is not by cowardice that Shylock is reduced, but by respect for the law. He was proud and resolute because of his conviction of his righteousness; when he no longer has the law on his side, he collapses. He has accepted Balthasar as a second Daniel, and, whatever she reveals the law to be, is law for him. "Is that the law?" he questions.[29] Shakespeare has maintained the unity of the character. As the law was Shylock's heart and soul, it is the cause of his destruction, and in this he attains to the dignity of tragedy. He is a dupe of the law. He has never reflected that the law might be a means to an end and hence only an instrument which might be variable in relation to that end, or that laws depend, at least in some measure, on human frailty. Portia has taken on the name of Balthasar; that was the name of Daniel in the court of Nebuchadnezzar.[30] She is a lawgiver who mediates between Belmont and Venice and harmonizes justice with law. She, according to Shakespeare, understands the limits of law. This is the poet's picture of the Jews—a people great by its devotion to the law but deceived by it.

Antonio, too, suffers from Portia's victory. She is aware that the ties which bind Bassanio to Antonio are strong. If Antonio had died, those ties would have poisoned Bassanio's life. She frees Bassanio from that onus, and then, with her deception concerning the rings, she forces Bassanio to admit explicitly the superiority of his love for Portia over everything else. She substitutes her lusty, gay, physical love for the gloomy, spiritual love that united Bassanio and Antonio. And Antonio is forced to speak up as guarantor for the new fidelity, which he had earlier challenged.[31]

V I

The conclusion of the trial is too unhappy a theme on which
to end a comedy. Venice is an unpleasant place, full of ugly
passions and unfulfilled hopes. It must be remembered that
Portia only plays the role of a *deus ex machina;* the ugly
truth remains that, if her improbable appearance had not
been made, revenge and blood would have been the result.
She has done nothing in principle to resolve the problems
which led to the war of Shylock and Antonio. And there is no
resolution. We can only hasten back to Belmont to forget
them.

Belmont is the seat of love; but it does not exist; it is a uto-
pia.[32] What is not possible in Venice is possible here. The
only love affair that takes place in Venice is a sordid one. Jessica, without the slightest trace of filial piety, remorselessly
leaves her father and robs him. She is one of the very few figures in Shakespeare who do not pay the penalty for their
crimes; and disobedience to one's parents, be they good or
bad, is a crime for Shakespeare; so is robbery. But somehow the atmosphere of Belmont changes all this. It is a place
where there are no laws, no conventions, no religions—just
men and women in love.

Jessica escapes to this never-never land with her Christian
lover and is saved.[33] Here the past is transformed in the glow
of Eros; the duties of everyday life appear the concerns of
drudges; duty is not the fulfillment of virtue, but the burden
of necessity. There is, indeed, a harmony in the world; it is
the harmony of the eternal order. In Venice, we forget this,
but Lorenzo reminds us in his great Platonic speech.[34] We
participate in one cosmos, and every soul is a reflection of
that cosmos. This is the harmony to which all men as men
can attain. But, because we are "grossly closed in" by a
"muddy vesture of decay," we cannot hear the music of the
spheres. It is only through the effect of music that we touch
from time to time on that higher world; and many men no
longer have any music in their souls. We are all human on a
high level and can have complete unity. But the accidents of
life force men into customs that cause them to forget the
whole and the immortal part of themselves; the nations have

no time for music. The ultimate harmony of men is a harmony, not on the level of their daily lives, but on that of a transcendence of them, an indifference to them, an assimilation to the movements of the spheres. Hence, humanity is attainable by only a few in rare circumstances, but it is potentially in all of us, and that is what makes us humans. The realization of Belmont does not solve the problems of Venice; it only mitigates their bleakness for those who understand. Portia, the goddess of love, can orchestrate a human harmony for a few.

Shakespeare does not understand Judaism, for he saw it from the outside; he looked at it, as no man rightfully can, from a purely political point of view. But he was personally less interested in the question of Judaism than in man's attempt to become man and man alone. He was of the conviction that it was of the nature of man to have varying opinions about the highest things and that such opinions become invested in doctrine and law and bound up with established interests. When confronted with one another, these opinions must quarrel. Such is life, and that must be accepted with manly resolution. In Venice and modern thought, there was an attempt to cut the Gordian knot and unite men, not on the level of their truly human sameness, but on that of the politically beneficial—a unity expressed in men's universal desire for gain. The consequences of this must be either conflict or a bastardization of all that is noble and true in each of the separate points of view. Venice had the adorned beauty of a strumpet. Shakespeare was not willing to sacrifice for this illusion the only true beauty, which lies somewhere beyond the heavens for the happy few.

NOTES

[1] For a typical and influential pre-Shakespearean evaluation of Venice, cf. Jean Bodin, *Les Six livres de la République* (Paris: 1577), pp. 726, 790. For the general understanding of Venice at the period, cf. Cardinal Gaspar Contareno, *The Commonwealth and Government of Venice* (London: 1599). Although the translation did not appear until five years after the production of *The Merchant of Venice*, the

book appeared in Italian in 1543, had been translated into French much before 1594, and was well known.

2 III. iii. 31-36; cp. IV. i. 39-43. All citations are to the Furness variorum edition (Philadelphia: J. B. Lippincott Co., 1888).

3 Shakespeare, unlike the earlier dramatists who presented Jews, seems to have gone to the Bible to find his characterizations rather than use a traditional image. His Jew is Jewish in his profession of faith; his principles are recognizable. It is similar with the Christian. Shakespeare seems to have taken a certain side of the Old Testament and added to it the criticism of the Jews made in the Pauline Epistles. One might look especially to Romans 9-11; the opposition between Shylock and Antonio might well be characterized as that between "a vessel of anger and a vessel of mercy." Or, more generally stated, the issue is precisely the quarrel between the Old Law and the New Law, each presenting its own evaluation of what is the most important element in piety and the morality consequent on piety. The two laws are related, but inimical. Shakespeare is, I believe, far more interested in Antonio's principles than in Shylock's. The Jews were not a problem in England; there were none, or practically none, and his audience was Christian. But Antonio's origins are somehow in Shylock's law, and he can only be seen in terms of those origins and his opposition to them. This is parallel to the New Testament's treatment of Jesus. The confrontation of the two is a re-enactment of the original confrontation, but altered and embittered by the unhappy history of fifteen hundred years. Cf. the dialogues between Antonio and Shylock (I. iii. 40-187; III. iii. 3-28; IV. i. 39-124).

4 IV. i. 150, 94-108; II. v. 30-40.

5 I. iii. 74-100.

6 I. i. 5-11, 98-109, 164-170; iii. 133-140; II. viii. 38-52; III. ii. 309-314; IV. i. 75-88, 120-124.

7 Mark 18:10-14. Shylock's righteousness in general parallels that of the Pharisee.

8 I. iii. 110-140.

9 II. ii. 2-29; III. v. 1-25. Launcelot carries his confusion further in his relations with his father, whom he respects and despises, thus mixing the responses of Portia and Jessica. His father, in this play which has so much to do with fathers, is blind. Launcelot, moreover, also parodies the loves between foreigners in this complicated world (III. v. 36-41).

10 I. iii. 33-39. Shylock's faith cuts him off from others; moreover, it gives him a different notion of the things that really count.

11 What causes Shylock to change his mind and go to eat with the Christians is unclear and can only be a subject of conjecture (II. v. 14-21). There is no indication that Antonio knew of the abduction (II. vi. 69-75). But Shylock takes it as a conspiracy known to and supported by the whole Christian world (III. i. 22-23).

12 II. viii. This scene not only describes a comic Shylock, but also gives a description of the parting of Bassanio and Antonio. This, too, in its way, has elements of the comic, although they are not intended by the speakers. It also reveals the pretense in Antonio's selflessness;

Bassanio is reminded of the risks his friend is taking for him when Antonio tells him to forget them. The scene cuts in both directions.

13 III. i. 32-34.

14 III. i. 75-123.

15 III. i. 115-116.

16 III. i. 47-66.

17 Shylock characteristically mentions laughter as a result of tickling. He and Antonio would not laugh at the same jokes.

18 Tubal, 10:2; Chus, 6; Jessica (Jesca), 11:29. The last two names are spelled otherwise in the King James version, but appear as they are here in the translations which follow the Greek of the Septuagint, and they were so spelled in translations at Shakespeare's time (cp. Note 30). "Shylock" poses a greater problem, and its origin can only be conjectured. But in the same passage is a name which comes closer to it than any other and is repeated six times (10:24; 11:12-15); it occurs both before and after the account of the Tower of Babel. This name appears as "Salah" in the King James, but is spelled "Shelah" (the last syllable is pronounced *ach*) in Hebrew, and so it appears in the English version of 1582. This is very close, indeed, and the Hebrew spelling of this name is almost the same as that of the only other Biblical name which has been suggested as a possible source: "Shiloh" (Genesis 19:10). Given that "Shelah" occurs in the same passage with the other names, it seems probable that he is Shylock's ancestor.

19 I. i. 175-176. The temple is mentioned at II. i. 50; Portia's use of religion is indicated in III. iv. 29-35. Portia would seem to be representative of classical *eros*. All myths and examples cited in Belmont are drawn from classical antiquity.

20 *Othello* I. iii. 280.

21 II. ix. 1-86.

22 The authority of the father is like that of the law and is supported by it. Both are binding and unmoving, and law gets its authority from the ancestral, from the fact that it was given by the fathers. Hence, Portia's experience with her father's law and what it means to her prepares her for dealing with the law in general—not as a lawyer, who by profession is committed to the law, but as one who stands outside the law and sees its relation to life and happiness. Shylock, on the other hand, simply takes his authority and his law for granted, or, otherwise stated, he identifies the law with the good.

23 III. iv. It is a man's world, but men are no longer able to control it, so the woman must become a man and restore the balance.

24 IV. i. 20-74. There is a strong resemblance between this scene and the accounts of the Crucifixion in the Gospels, with the role of the Duke paralleling that of Pilate (cf. Matthew 27:17-23; Mark 15: 8-15; Luke 23:13-25). Shylock's insistence that Antonio die and his unwillingness to say why are parallel to the Jews' conduct in relation to Jesus. Without Portia, the conclusion would have also been similar.

25 IV. i. 120-124. Antonio seeks martyrdom; Portia will not allow it to him.

[26] Portia gives the appearance of total indifference to persons which is proper to the law: "Which is the Merchant here? and which the Jew?" (IV. i. 181). But she has prepared her case, and it is a discriminatory one. Shylock transfers his devotion from the religious law to the civil law: law as law is respectable to him. This is Portia's great insight.

[27] IV. i. 207-211. "Therefore Jew . . . we do pray for mercy." The Lord's Prayer (Matthew 6:9) is meant to be a distillation of common Jewish teachings. The specific teaching about mercy is frequently referred to Ecclesiasticus 28.

[28] IV. i. 397-419.

[29] IV. i. 329.

[30] Daniel 1:7. In the King James version, the name is Belshazzar, but it was frequently spelled "Balthasar," following the Greek (cp. Note 18, supra).

[31] V. i. 273-280; cp. IV. i. 296-303, 469-471. The obviously erotic symbolism of the rings contrasts the basis of Portia's power over Bassanio with that of Antonio's.

[32] It is literally nowhere; it is unknown in Italy. I take it to be the elaboration of men's prayers; that best place which indicates the perfection which is unattainable in ordinary life, with its accidents and necessities. Etymologically, it is "beautiful mountain." Could it be Parnassus?

[33] V. i. 1-22. On the first level, it is clearly Jessica's conversion that saves her. But other difficulties are overcome by the magic of the place. At the beginning of their scene in the garden, Jessica and Lorenzo recite a list of unhappy lovers separated by parents or the opposition of nations.

[34] V. i. 63-98. Cf. Plato Republic x. 616d-617d and John Burnet, "Shakespeare and Greek Philosophy," Essays and Addresses (London: Chatto & Windus, 1926).

3

✦❀✦❀✦❀✦❀✦❀✦❀✦❀✦❀✦❀✦❀✦❀✦❀✦❀✦❀✦

Cosmopolitan Man and the Political Community

᪥ *OTHELLO* ᪥

IN THE WORLD of today, the existence of a common humanity has been established, negatively at least, by a common fear of a common extinction. Only rational beings fear thermonuclear annihilation; only rational beings can create such means of annihilation. An unprecedented danger supplies a new kind of evidence for the oldest thesis in political philosophy: man is by nature a rational and political animal. The roots of man's humanity, as of his inhumanity, are in the political community and in the political community's capacity for making war or peace. As the growth from the roots reaches what were once the heavens, the problem of reconciling the origins with the ends attains an acute proportion. Can the new awareness of the commonness of our common humanity cause the fashioning of institutions and men equal to the problem that that very humanity has created? Can the particularity that characterizes individual races, nations, creeds—the particularity that has, from the known origins of political life until the present, provided the substance of political life both in its misery and in its glory—can that particularity transform itself into universality, as the finest and ultimate fruit of human reason? Or may the consummation of rationality, as it is given us to know it, be found in its own self-extinction?

Shakespeare's explicit treatment of the possibility of an interracial, interfaith society is given its most detailed development in his two Venetian plays, two plays which may well be thought the profoundest recorded analysis of the relation of Jew and Christian, of white man and black man. Whether Shakespeare's apparent pessimism is the final word on this subject we need not here pronounce. Certainly no further apology is needed to introduce an attempt to comprehend, in human and political terms, the grounds for that pessimism.

I

The Earl of Shaftesbury, in the most penetrating criticism of *Othello* that I have read,[1] asserts that the marriage of Othello and Desdemona is a mismatch, a monstrous union founded on the lying pretensions of a charlatan and the unhealthy imagination of a misguided young girl. For him, the tragedy is not the consequence of Iago's vile machinations, but the natural fruit of seeds that are sown in the characters of the heroes and in their relationship. The simple, citizen's moral of the story is, according to Shaftesbury, that such marriages between foreigners who have nothing in common other than their desire for novelty are to be avoided and condemned. Only the sick taste of one not satisfied at home could have led Desdemona to her choice; only a moral education that did not move the fantasy and the sympathy of the girl could account for her blind search for the incredible and the exotic. Shaftesbury, echoing the moral taste of the pre-Romantic critics, sees the denouement as the just punishment of faulty beings.

However narrow this understanding of the play may be, it raises in a direct and honest fashion the fundamental question: what is the character of the relationship between Desdemona and Othello? The interpretation of *Othello* has tended to neglect the question and has concentrated on the psychological development of the jealousy. But this jealousy has no meaning except in relation to the kind of man who suffers it and the reasons why he is particularly susceptible to it. We are presented with the picture of a couple who have married in an unusual way but who are nonetheless very much in love and who are led to disaster through the external actions of a hostile world. We are asked to believe that a paragon of strength and confidence is transformed into a furious beast driven by suspicion only because he has been tempted by a devil. It is not enough to say that such is the nature of jealousy; we can easily imagine many men, exposed to the same temptations, who would never have succumbed to them. Even the most superficial reader is struck by the slightness of the proofs which convince Othello of Desdemona's infidelity. Is not Othello ripe for the doubt which comes to afflict him? Are we to believe that the jealousy which erupts so unexpectedly is not the fruit of a soil long prepared and cultivated, albeit unconsciously? Does not Shakespeare always incorporate into the life of each of his tragic heroes precisely those elements which make him the aptest vehicle for the emergence of that phenomenon which he, above all others, exhibits?

The latter alternative is clearly the correct one, for it alone is in conformity with what we know of Shakespeare's genius and of the nature of tragedy in general. In other Shakespearean tragedies, disaster develops directly from the character of the tragic hero and, even more, out of precisely those features of it that constitute his greatness. Macbeth's pride and ambition, which raise him above other men in daring and vision, are the direct cause of his murder of Duncan and his entry on a tyrant's career. Macbeth's crimes are consequences of Macbeth's greatness of soul, and the enormous impact of the play comes from the impression of overpowering force conveyed by the hero joined to our sense of the inevitability of his destiny. Or consider Hamlet's responsibility for the deaths of all those he loved and the failure of his attempt to do justice. Is it not bound up with those traits that cause us to admire him—his conscience and his admirable sensitivity to his fellows? If this were not the case, we should either regard these men simply as criminals or as beings who may deserve our pity, but they would certainly not move our deepest emotions or call forth our respect. As it is, we see them as examples of human greatness; they move in areas of experience from which ordinary mortals are cut off. But this very superiority in human quality seems to lead to crime and disaster. It is this combination that constitutes the unique quality of tragedy.

Which virtues, then, make Othello's jealousy necessary and in some measure excuse it? Why must the great general with the sovereign self-control murder his innocent wife? Because Iago told him she was unfaithful? This is to degrade the work to the level of psychological "realism," a realism which contents itself with the analysis of passions, no matter by whom they are felt or to what end. It is to deny that Shakespeare regarded his heroes' emotions as truly interesting only insofar as the one who experiences them is worthy of attention and his objects serious. In this perspective, Othello appears a weak fool and Desdemona's death a senseless slaughter that can evoke only horror and disgust. Tragedy is founded on the notion that, in the decisive respect, human beings are free and responsible, that their fates are the consequences of their choices. All that is a result of external force or chance is dehumanizing in the tragic view. But *Othello* so interpreted is only the story of an easily inflamed man who has the unfortunate accident of meeting an Iago. This does not do justice to the sentiment we have in seeing the play, and it is the task of interpretation to render articulate what is only felt and to elaborate the larger significance of the characters and the action. Such an analysis requires more attention to the political setting of the drama than has been the habit.

I I

To this end, we must go behind the jealousy to the strange love that united Othello and Desdemona. It is in their love that the seeds of the ultimate disaster are sown. It is not an easy union to analyze, this marriage between an old, black, foreign warrior and a young, beautiful, innocent Venetian noblewoman. In fact, the first act is devoted almost exclusively to development of the character of the marriage and its ambiguity. The suggestions as to the source of the union include lust, profit, and the purest admiration for virtue. In a sense, the entire play is motivated by the beliefs of the actors about the nature of the love, and it is these beliefs much more than any acts that are the moving causes of the tragedy. Indeed, one of the unique characterististics of *Othello* is that the final action of the play is so little the result of previous actions and so much the consequence of changes in opinion wrought in the characters during the play. Perhaps the best way to see what these opinions are is through the activities of Iago.

Iago is a villain, no doubt, but his villainy is not shallow; he has a clear grasp of what is most important to everyone (with the possible exception of Emilia), and he acts on all the persons only through their own opinions. In each case, the individual can be justly regarded as responsible for his own troubles; Iago only precipitates something that was already there. He works like a confidence man; only the quality intrinsic to the one he tempts enables him to succeed.[2] He is a faithful mirror of all around him; he adapts himself to those with whom he speaks. In a sense, we would not know the other characters in the play without Iago. We would see them only as they appear in ordinary life, without penetrating the masks that conceal their real natures. Iago alone lets us know from the outset those weaknesses in others that would otherwise stand unrevealed until the crises of their lives. Iago shows the hidden necessity in men, the things they care about most; he has a diabolic insight. He offers men what they hope for or are afraid of, and, in so doing, he causes their characters to undergo the extreme test. For example, it is possible that Roderigo might have forgotten Desdemona and married someone else. But, in appealing to Roderigo's defeated suit, in offering him hope, Iago makes him display his petty and absurd nature, full of spite and envy, capable of extreme folly and crime in a spirit of innocent stupidity. Roderigo is such a fool as thinks he can buy the favors of a queen. Iago is only the catalyst of Roderigo's folly. If Roderigo had not come to ruin, his salvation would have been sheer accident. Now, Iago proposes as his supreme task to encompass the downfall of Othello; and it is through Iago's actions and speech that we can see his catalytic agency on Othello and thereby see the necessity which shapes the tragic end.

The play begins in an atmosphere of conspiracy, and our first acquaintance with Othello is through the eyes of an enemy. The beginning is a sort of foretaste of Iago's skill, showing him expertly manipulating Roderigo. Iago is arranging the disclosure of the marriage to Brabantio; he wishes to present it in such a way that "though that his joy be joy," [3] the union will appear to be an abomination. In the midst of a horrendous hue and cry, the love affair is made known to Brabantio as a species of robbery motivated by lust. The father of Desdemona is presented with the most obscene picture of his daughter's relations with Othello. Any chance that Brabantio might accept the marriage is destroyed by his first view of it. His mind is automatically closed to the possibility that it may be a special and fine sort of relationship. Of course, like all Iago's victims, he is predisposed toward the insinuated interpretation.

He is a good Venetian, a solid man of importance and property.[4] For him, the best is at home, is Venetian. There is law and order in Venice, and the Venetian ways are *the* standard of conduct. Any other way, anything foreign, may be tolerated or even admired, but can never be fully equal. He is a model of good citizenship, and, as does any father, he expects to find in his wonderful daughter what he believes is best in himself. His daughter is his fullest reality. Hence, her defection from Venetian standards is a reflection on him and on Venice. He can only regard it as the effect of magic; she is his daughter, so there must be something wrong with her or with him—both of which alternatives are repugnant. Therefore, the cause must be something supernatural. Brabantio is not a man particularly inclined to superstition; all to the contrary. He is a very sober and reasonable man. His reasonableness is that of a good burgher who cannot see much that goes beyond the local and the evident; to admit the possibility that there are important dimensions beyond these would destroy the very reasonableness which enables him to operate so effectively within his own little world. He refers to drugs where his modern counterpart might lay the blame on "foreign philosophies." His speech to Othello is a masterpiece of common sense, revealing the virtues and defects of that faculty. He refers himself again and again to things of sense, to what is palpable.[5] He cannot conceive of a relationship based on spiritual communion alone, devoid of the ordinary attractions; or, to put it more favorably for him, he cannot imagine that a match of such alien beings could be purely spiritual. It is, as he says, a relation that braves nature, years, country, credit, everything.[6] He poses the question very clearly: what can possibly be the basis of their love?

We are thus presented with two explicit choices and one that is implied: either the marriage is caused by brutal lust, occult practices, or—as the spectator might infer—something beautiful and fine not common to the commerce of the species. Every dramatic device has been employed by Shakespeare to give expression to the opposition between Othello and Desdemona and the shocking character of their marriage. To an Elizabethan audience, the extraordinary nature of this relationship was doubly clear. Although racial prejudice did not exist in the modern sense nor as it does in America with its special political history, there was perhaps a livelier sense of the differences among nations, races, and religions. The world was larger and less uniform, and there were still fundamental differences in belief, taste, and desire from people to people. There was less contact between the various nations and a strong sense of the barbarism of those who lay beyond one's own borders—a sense kept alive by the occasional presence of certain types of foreigner. Moreover, there was no liberal ideology which constrained intelligent citizens to suppress or alter their first feelings toward foreigners or those of another color in favor of an attitude based on reflection or abstract conviction, rather than emotion. And there were no compelling political reasons for the attempt to eradicate distinctions between races, creeds, and nations. Hence, Othello's exotic qualities were sharpened for the audience for which the play was intended. Shakespeare chose the most visible and striking means to arouse the sentiments of the spectators—Othello's blackness.[7]

Othello's color not only provides a visual contrast, but is meant to horrify the viewer. Whether Shakespeare personally felt that this was only an English prejudice is not here at issue. What is clear is that Othello is physically repulsive to the other figures in the play and that "black Othello" set next to "fair Desdemona" is meant to arouse those who see it. It is not that there would be any racist principle against their being married or that Othello would be regarded as an inferior being because he is not white; it is rather that he would not be considered a normal or appropriate choice for a young beauty's romantic interest. Iago knows that it is the common opinion that Othello is ugly, and the working of his poison depends decisively on his manipulation of this opinion. It is the necessary condition of Roderigo's foolish belief that Desdemona will grant his suit, of Othello's stinging doubts about his own attractiveness, of Brabantio's assumption that there has been an ugly seduction. Brabantio bases his whole appeal to the duke on the evident incredibility of Desdemona's being aroused physically by "a thing such as" Othello.[8] In the theater, where the imagination is limited by the physical presence of the characters, there is a tendency, as in painting, to infer the moral worth of persons from the way they look; in such circumstances, Othello's blackness must have an overwhelming effect and be a predisposing factor difficult to overcome. In *Titus Andronicus*, the relation of Aaron the Moor with Tamara, queen of the Goths, is meant to strike one immediately as foul and appropriate only to barbarians. And Portia's reaction to the "complexion" of the Prince of the Moors certainly expressed what all Elizabethans felt. She is painted as having healthy tastes, and with her Moorish suitor she was running the risk of being permanently coupled to something very unattractive.

The color difference is not all that is meant to move the audience to grave reservations about Othello. There is the fact that he is a Moor. The Moors were popularly considered barbarous, heathens naturally at war with Christians and Europeans. They were understood to be dangerous and unaware of the limitations set by civilized man. The villainous Aaron proves that this way of looking at Moors was not totally unknown to Shakespeare; he could present this scoundrel as plausible without the preparation that is necessary to convince us that Othello is noble. And the other Moor in Shakespeare, the prince in *The Merchant of Venice*, is treated as a comic and absurd figure. He has many traits in common with Othello, especially his warlike nature and talk of his adventures; he is presented somewhat as Iago would like to present Othello.[9] In sophisticated European circles, he appears ridiculous and "stuffed with epithets of war." To the untutored English audience, the Moor was a stranger bringing from his dark continent mysteries, dangers, and a new religion. Shakespeare, in making a Moor his hero, runs counter to an established pattern of thought. He must make special efforts to convince us of Othello's nobility and superior humanity. But, in so doing he does not intend enlightenment, as Lessing does in *Nathan the Wise*. For Shakespeare's Moor, after making all the detours of civilized man and manifesting an unexpected depth, returns at the end to the barbarism that the audience originally expected. The first, primitive prejudice against Othello seems to find justification in the conclusion.

In addition to the two major considerations which make the match so unsuitable—color and nation—there are age, wealth, and social station.[10] We should bear in mind the fact that marriage had a somewhat different status for the Elizabethans than it has for us. As heirs of the Romantic tradition, we believe that love is enough to justify all, and our sympathies go out to it. But, formerly, marriages were arranged. Fathers were thought apt to have a more balanced view of what a lifetime's living together would require than did their inexperienced children in their passing fancies. The responsibilities of family and the continuance of great traditions had to be taken into consideration. The marriage of Othello and Desdemona neglected all of these things in violating the wishes of Brabantio. What predisposes us immediately in favor of Othello—that he is beloved of Desdemona despite his alien birth and color—must have given pause to Shakespeare's audience. If this is not taken into consideration, Othello seems the victim of merciless persecution, and his greatness and weakness are lost to our eyes. It is against this background that Shakespeare tells his story.

Indeed, the absence of the ordinary external accompaniments of marriage suggests that this is a marriage of true love. It differs from conventional marriages, supported by money, beauty, and similarity of position and education. A love purified of all accidental and physical elements would certainly be a great human achievement, a transcendence of mundane attachments. It would be a love of the true, rather than of the familiar. But can marriage exist in such a rarefied atmosphere? Once marriage is purged of conventional dross, what really remains? What is the cause of the love of Othello and Desdemona? It is certain that Othello gave her no drugs and that Iago's lascivious description of their romance is false, designed to shock refined sentiment. Othello may well be entirely past the stage of caring for physical pleasures ("the young affects in me defunct"; "to be free and bounteous to her mind"),[11] and, if the marriage ever reached consummation, it was not before Cyprus. Not even Desdemona regards Othello as physically desirable.[12] Putting aside for a moment the notion that she was just a silly, inexperienced child and Othello a fortune-hunter,[13] their relation would appear to be an example of what has come to be known as a platonic love—a love not lacking in passion, rather one of the most intense passion, but completely beyond physical need, based on mutual admiration. This raises the question of what precisely was admired by each.

Brabantio assumed that Venice would come to the aid of Venice outraged, in the shape of his daughter. But, as Iago knew very well, *raison d'état* made Othello necessary and would overrule any claim made against him.[14] Who is this Othello who is so important to Venice that he can stand against the attacks of its most powerful and respected citizens, so eminent that he eclipses Brabantio himself, to the point that the duke no longer notices the senator when they enter together? Othello is the protector of Venice, a foreigner brought in to ward off the attacks of other foreigners, the Turks. The Turks are men of another religion; so was Othello. But he is a convert to Christianity and is most loyal to it; it provides much of his fervor for the cause of Venice.

As he is first represented to us, he appears well worthy of his reputation and of the trust reposed in him. He seems a man of simple decency who imposes on others by his quiet strength and evident competence. He is most impressive in his confidence in himself, an apparent sureness of his worth that nothing can shake. He bears up under abuse with a dignity that makes his attackers seem mean and small and gives the immediate impression that the right is on his side. He maintains all proportions, a respect for Brabantio's age and worth, while never losing the dignity of his conviction that he himself is just, a conviction so surely held that it needs no protest. He is certain that his real services are appreciated by the city and that he is esteemed. Moreover, his ancestry is royal, and he is hence of a dignity equal to that of any Venetian. He is apparently not the uprooted foreigner unsure of his status in the world. In a word, he is self-sufficient, according to his own belief. The most amazing fact of the play is that from this acme of assurance emerges the nadir of suspicion. There is an almost unbelievable transformation, and it is Shakespeare's analysis of this development that contains the deepest meaning of the play.

How, then, did the love affair come to pass? Surprisingly enough, not through the deeds of Othello, but through his speeches. Although he protests himself to be only a man of action and lacking in eloquence, his influence over Desdemona has its source in the terrible tales of his past. Othello represents himself as a poor speaker and one who depreciates mere words. But he seems to influence others almost entirely through his speeches. He is impressive for what he is supposed to have done, but his own testimony is the only real source for our belief in those great actions. He gives witness to his own might and is believed.[15] In his great speech recounting the course of his wooing, he makes it seem that it was the gentle Desdemona who made the advances and that he was the wooed. Desdemona admired him for his incredible deeds and his great sufferings. He loved her because she pitied him; he loved her for her love of him, which is a sort of confirmation of his own worth. He is lovable for his sufferings, and pity is the source of her love. This presentation of the love affair is in harmony with Othello's self-sufficiency. He is admirable and needs little beyond himself. Desdemona is the crowning acquisition of a virtuous life. The relationship is a sound one because Othello is a man in possession of himself, of notable quality, and Desdemona cares for someone both solid and noble.

III

The course of the play, however, makes clear that Othello is not so firmly established as he may appear to be or as he believes himself to be. To understand why, we must reflect for a moment on the character of the political community, as it naturally is, always and everywhere. Civil society is a closed corporation; those who live in it have certain bonds that they do not share with those whom they call foreigners. The situation is similar to that of the family, and in fact the political community is often understood as a sort of family. It may be a mere accident that a man is born in one place rather than another. But that accident may be decisive in forming him. Each city has its manners and its gods; the very life of the city depends on this particularism: to live, it must defend its ancestral way, which is a combination of human accidents and special institutions adapted to the here and now. Good citizenship implies a devotion to those ways; a universality, a cosmopolitanism that devoted itself to the essence of man as he is eternally, would destroy those roots of affection which are necessary to political life. Practical life requires adaptations to particular and imperfect circumstances and emphasizes considerations which are theoretically indifferent. To live as men, acting men, humankind must be divided, the distinction between friend and stranger must come into being, and men must care more for their fellow citizens and their city than they do for all others. Just as no one can become truly a member of a family into which he was not born, no one can set his roots deeply in a city that is not his own. In a sense, the brotherhood of man does not extend beyond the walls of the city. Or there are two brotherhoods of man—one as men are universally and the other as men are in their practical lives—the two being incommensurable. A man can be fully at home only in his own city. His style of life and his goals are provided by it; from it he gets his sense of belonging and his knowledge of what he is in the world. Most, if not all, men know themselves from their place in the city; their notions of what is right and wrong and what is respectable are part of this whole. A being who was completely indifferent to such a world, who had no need of any particular place, would either be a beast living on unconscious passion or a superman, a sort of deity, who could receive his laws and his aspirations from the silent vastness of the universe.[16]

Othello seems to feel at home in Venice. But how could this foreigner, who is also black, arrive at such a station? There seem to be several immediate possibilities. We can set aside the alternative that he did not care about the opinion of others. He insists on respect; his very killing of Desdemona, he says, he did for his honor. He feels it necessary to point out that his background is as good as that of any Venetian.[17] He is a proud man, and pride does not brook contempt. The truly proud man considers himself superior to others because he is above the petty concerns of private interest and can devote himself to the common good; his rewards are in the glory he reaps from other men. Reputation is the stuff of his being. Othello believes that he deserves admiration and that he has it, that Venice is truly grateful to him for his services.[18] His virtue outweighs the accident of his birth. Othello believes that he is universally valued and valuable, that he can go any place and be accepted; the walls of the city are not really boundaries to virtue. At the same time, he can only see himself in the opinions of the men about him; this is the contradiction in his situation—he is independent of particular national ways of life, but he draws his being, like any citizen, from the honors accorded by the cities, honors which differ from city to city and which are generally reserved for citizens. Is it really possible to transcend the city on the level of the life of action lived in it and become universal? Can a man who has no "natural" home be a statesman? [19]

Othello's problem is best illustrated by the fact that he is a mercenary. Mercenaries are traditionally regarded as a low form of humanity. They sell their courage to the highest bidder; what is noble in a citizen becomes in them a form of baseness. The citizen risks his being for the sake of the laws; the laws lend him their dignity, and he is exalted in his devotion to something beyond his own life. A mercenary is indifferent to the very thing which gives meaning to the citizen's soldiering; he does not truly care for what he is defending. The glory that attaches to heroism is not given those who are better able to kill men than others; to be above the animal or the perverse, the death of men must be understood as the sacrifice of life in the name of some cause greater than life. Even if a mercenary desired to fight nobly, he could not, for he cannot care as the citizen cares for what is his own. Nor is it in the nature of men to serve freely those who will not honor them. Hence it is that mercenaries are degraded men who make a travesty of the highest acts of citizenship.

But Othello is not such an insensitive being, lacking in the dignity which refuses to sell life for money. He is a man who identifies himself with his warring and who, as we have said, demands respect for his worth. How is he able to make himself so Venetian? It is surely, in part, his Christianity that is responsible. He is engaged in a war against the Turks, and he believes that the unity of true Christians is a kind of brotherhood, a brotherhood of such an overpowering influence that local differences pale into insignificance. He has something of the character of a Christian knight-errant, going from place to place, honored and worthwhile wherever men hold the faith. (It is important to remark that Othello is born a stranger to Christianity as well as to Venice. In respect to both religion and race, he is by birth closer to the Turks.) The local—the political, in the ancient sense—does not weigh so heavily on a man in the Christian context.

This community of faith allows Othello to fight his war and care about its purposes without assuming the comic aspect of the outsider who interests himself in what is none of his business or the vulgar one of the hired agent. The faith provides a cosmopolitanism which is not limited by the accident of birth, the peculiarity of education, or the difference in social position. The importance of Othello's Christianity, both for his own sense of dignity and purpose and for the possibility of his stepping over boundaries that would otherwise have been insuperable, cannot be overestimated. If Christianity is really the one most needful thing, then he who is its defender deserves honor and reverence, and within its universal unity there are no strangers. Othello's last words recall again that he is one of the best of the faithful; if he is attached to Venice, it is because he can regard the city as an instrument of the faith.[20]

But it is questionable whether Othello is venerated as

much as he thinks or in the way that he thinks. He believes that he is cared for as a citizen is cared for—that there are not two standards of affection and justice, one for those who belong and one for those who are outside. Othello does not consider himself a means, a tool in the hands of Venice, but an end, a being worthwhile in himself. Yet we find him at the beginning of the play having been out of employment for nine months. Iago believes that Othello is used only because, at the moment, there is no one else to command.[21] And there is the overwhelming fact that, as soon as the victory is achieved, Othello is cashiered. There is little question but that he is used sparingly and only for the pressing needs of Venice; he is not a citizen.[22] But, further, it is of the utmost importance to understand that he is not so much the best general as reputed to be the best general. The duke says this.[23] Othello is a man of great reputation, and, as Iago makes clear, there is a decisive difference between reputation and true deserving.[24] Othello is trusted; but in the play we are given no examples of his prowess, unlike the men of action portrayed in other plays. His only military success is the result of chance, of a *tempest*. For it, he proclaims a victory, and his reputation is thereby enhanced. But he is not actually responsible for the victory proclaimed. Desdemona loves him for his stories. He is, as Iago says, a great talker of war.

I do not suggest that Othello had never done anything to deserve his reputation; I only point out that we are never given any direct testimony or evidence of what he did, whereas we are given to see that he imposes himself on others by his reputation. He seems to be a case of men's need for a hero. Every city and every army needs leaders, and those leaders, in order to command, must be respected and even idolized. No matter what their merit, in order to feel the confidence that is necessary to the dangerous enterprise of war, they must be invested with authority. Around them spring up myths, not created by them, but arising from the popular need. So that they can subordinate themselves to their leaders, the people endow them with superhuman merits. Othello is a man on whom "opinion throws a more safer voice," and opinion is a "sovereign mistress of effects." He is known to the duke to be valuable because he is generally well thought of. Othello is sure of himself because he is respected; he is respected so that others can be confident in danger. It is a circle which is not grounded in a reality free from opinion.

For Othello, this means that, if the opinions change, he is lost, for he has no source of confidence outside a city that is not his own city. His Christianity proves to be not enough to overcome the primeval and necessary prejudices of civil society. In some measure, his very character depended on his ignorance of the source of his strength. He assumed that his reputation was deserved and was secure. To the extent that he felt this, he could be at home in Venice. There was no tension between his foreignness, his universality, and his need for Venetian and hence local opinion in which to see himself as in a glass. To use his practical abilities as a warrior, Othello needed a home, a place for which he could fight meaningfully, and this required a reputation. The argument of the play is that such reputations are only given grudgingly and conditionally to foreigners. Yet Othello could never accept this and still be able to fight in the citizen's, or proud man's, spirit. The massiveness of his self-assurance in the face of the tenuousness of his real position shows that his life is based on a critical lack of self-knowledge.

Othello, though radically dependent, represents himself as completely independent; and the myth of his independence seems to be less for his own benefit than for the sake of those who made him. They could not trust him if they knew him to be their own creation. The very end of the creation requires that the knowledge that it was creation and not discovery be forgotten. This is a necessary self-deception without which the purposes of myth-making would be frustrated. All might have succeeded, there might have been no revelation of Othello's true situation, if he had not gone one step too far in the direction of his conquest of Venice. That step was his falling in love with Desdemona and marrying her. In Desdemona, he had chosen the fairest flower of one of the best families in Venice. In marrying her, he seemed to prove that he was fully lovable in Venice by Venetians, that he had fully naturalized himself. In the manner of his wooing, he continues the masquerade that not he but Desdemona is the one who needs; she is the lover, and he the beloved.[25] He is still the independent being to whom others come because of his qualities. But Iago knows that this is not true. It is his awareness of Othello's absolute dependence on Desdemona, of which Othello himself is totally unaware, that allows Iago to bring about the destruction which he plots.

I V

Love, according to the classical analysis, means imperfection, need. The motion of one being toward another, the recognition of something admirable in another, implies the lack of something in the one admiring.[26] What a man desires to possess, he does not already possess. The desire to possess another human being implies that qualities belonging to the beloved object are lacking to the lover. Hence, a perfect being would not love, because he would possess all that is admirable within himself; there would be no sufficient reason for him to go outside himself. He who pretends to love without needing is an impostor. The lover admits by his very love a dependence on and, in this sense, an inferiority to, his beloved. The beloved, as beloved, does not return love; the man who is loved for his learning does not love the lover for his ignorance. If he returns love at all, he does so for some other reason—because the lover has some other virtue which in his turn makes him an object of love. One who loves does not, for that reason, have any claim on the affections of the one he loves; on the contrary, he has, in loving, made an admission of imperfection which the beloved is under no obligation to reciprocate. The beloved has the privileged position, and the lover, if his affection is not returned, must become conscious of unworthiness and begin to lack confidence in himself. His value as a human being is called into question, but he has no right to complain, for love is not a question of duty.

Nonetheless, every lover desires to be loved in return, for only by the return of love can he possess the beloved, and, moreover, his self-esteem is at stake. He has, at the moment he committed himself, become dependent on another for his self-esteem. At the same time, he has made his situation doubly difficult by having to some extent admitted himself to be undeserving by the fact of loving. Othello is unaware of his need for Desdemona; he believes that she loves him, and he is secure in his estimate of himself. But he truly loves her love and requires it for his very existence. He says that he is no more when he is unloved. Iago discerns this; Othello, says Iago, would renounce his baptism for her: "her appetite shall play the god with his weak function." [27] At Othello's first glimmerings of recognition of his situation, he says, "When I love thee not, chaos is come again." The world in which he lives was created by his love and is dependent on the continuation of that love. Iago's success is based on his making Othello realize both his attachment to Desdemona and that this attachment does not necessarily deserve a recompense. Othello now needs a proof of love to justify his own existence. The whole house of cards in which he has lived starts to tumble. [28]

When Othello begins to need the proof of love, he also begins to realize that proofs of love may be impossible to come by, especially for "great ones," toward whom those in inferior positions are likely to use all the wiles of persuasion and deception. Except by the omniscient, the motions of the human soul cannot be observed. Acts are never proof, because they are ambiguous, especially in matters of love. One can never know for certain what another thinks of him, and, when that knowledge is required, the quest for certainty can be the cruelest of torments to which a human being can be subjected. Iago makes this clear to Othello in masterful fashion, first by refusing to tell him what he knows about Cassio and Desdemona, while claiming that even a slave is free as to his innermost thoughts. [29] As love can only be free, nature has so constructed man that his loves and hates can be hidden from observation—a concealment which is the precondition of freedom. Then Iago, with prodigious obscenity, shocking the most revered beliefs and presenting him with pictures of the realization of his most dreaded fears, shows him that one can never tell what an act means. [30]

It is at this point that jealousy becomes dominant and triumphs. *Othello* is admittedly the story of a jealous man, and it is in the analysis of the origin and the consequences of this terrible passion that the play fulfills itself. Jealousy is in itself a passion of the weak and the contemptible, or so it is generally believed to be. The other characters who suffer it in the play—Roderigo, Iago, and Bianca—are base figures. So it is that, when the confident Othello becomes a victim of jealousy, his tragedy is already complete; he has lost all that which he was or pretended to be. Nonetheless, in spite of its intrinsic pettiness, jealousy takes on a certain grandeur when it occurs in a man of Othello's proportions; the size and depth of his hopes lend themselves to his sense of loss, and his furies are in proportion to the nobility of his deceived ambitions. Moreover, jealousy as traditionally understood was not always a contemptible and ridiculous passion.

There was one great example of it which, if it could not stand as a model for others' imitation, gave a certain cosmic significance to the passion—the God of the Old Testament who commands love and promises revenge unto the third and fourth generation for those who are not obedient.[31] Although God's jealousy cannot be an object of human imitation and far transcends the disappointment of deceived husbands, it could not help but add significance to the jealousy of ordinary mortals. God's anger at those who transgress the commandment has a similarity to the anger of men who are deceived; to understand what God's jealousy is, men must begin from the only experience of jealousy they have, i.e., human jealousy. And, with the sanctity brought to marriage by Judaism and Christianity, even the motives take on a certain similarity; the jealous husband takes a just vengeance for the violation of a sacred commandment. The husband is made in the image of the Lord.

This is not to say that the Old Testament God justifies human jealousy; it is only that His jealousy gives jealousy in general a significance it would not have in a non-Biblical context. It would be difficult to imagine a Greek tragedy whose hero is primarily characterized by the false suspicion of his wife's infidelity; this would be a subject of comedy. Shakespeare has succeeded in this *tour de force* because the enlarged sense of the word "jealousy" unconsciously affects our perception of those who suffer it. Shakespeare's Othello does act out on the human scene a god's role;[32] he is a universal stranger, a leader who can command and punish wherever he goes. He insists on honor and wreaks bloody vengeance on those who disobey. Shakespeare analyzes the sophistry of the heart of a man who tries to be thus divine.

This stranger from Africa comes to Venice, in a gentle guise, insisting on nothing from anyone. He takes the respect and affection given him as free gift and is himself a lover. But from his love emerges jealousy and an insistence more intense than could have previously been imagined. Jealousy, as Iago says, is doubt. It is the accompaniment of love that is unrequited or suspected of being so. Jealousy implies a lack of self-assurance. The man who knows he is worthy of love will not be jealous; if his wife is unfaithful, he will no longer deem her worthy of his love. He is himself the touchstone; this is precisely the attitude that Othello thinks he must take and says he will take.[33] He will forget Desdemona. Jealousy is contemptible because it bespeaks imperfection; he who suffers it must think either himself unlovable or the one he loves corrupt; but he nevertheless continues to love and think it right to love and be loved.

Jealousy rarely, if ever, sees itself as jealousy. Rather is it reflected in the soul it possesses as justice. The revenge worked by jealousy is said to be the desert of the victim. She was unfaithful. But is being unfaithful necessarily a crime, if the one who insists on love does not deserve it? A man who passes sentence in his own interest, for the sake of preserving what is his own or punishing what refuses to be his, is not a judge but a tyrant. He insists that love be given. But only conformity, not love, can be gained by force; love is a free gift. A love which insists on return is violence. However that may be, the jealous man cannot admit that it is jealousy that motivates him, for he would then confess himself to be acting for himself and contrary to the interests of those he judges. He must pretend that he has been wronged, that he truly deserved love. And the proof of deserving love is being loved.

Othello appears as a judge. Indeed, his only actions in the play are judgments. We have two such examples, the comparison of which is instructive for our understanding of Othello's real claims. Those judgments are of Cassio and Desdemona. His judgment of Cassio is, in a way, a preparation for that of Desdemona. It gives us a hint of Othello's merits and limitations as judge.

Cassio, inveigled by Iago into drinking, causes a disturbance. Othello arrives on the scene. He is completely in com-

mand and assumes that all will bend to his least word or gesture; his jealousy has not yet risen.[34] He summarily dismisses
Cassio. To do so is perfectly correct from the point of view
of human justice. Cassio is a soldier and has been drinking
before going on duty. The unfortunate circumstances that led
him into trouble do not excuse him from the responsibilities
of an officer. But Shakespeare has presented the scene in
such a way that we know that, from the point of view of complete justice, this is a miscarriage. Cassio has been duped
and has been made to appear fully responsible. The real cul-
prit is Iago. Othello is a decent general doing justice on the
basis of acts done. He does not try to pry into hidden motives. He judges by the surface. Every judge must believe
that he knows the principles of justice and that he is personally disinterested in those judged. He must have some
source of knowledge which he believes to be certain, or he
could not in conscience judge other men. Judges receive this
knowledge from the law. Othello proceeds with Cassio according to the rules of military discipline. These rules are
limited in scope. Yet they express what all would admit is a
true form of justice, the limits of which are due to the limited
nature of their purpose—military discipline—and not to par-
tiality or hypocrisy.

The judgment of Desdemona is in sharp contrast with this.
Here, Othello judges, not external actions, but intentions,
the innermost movements of a soul. He does not need proof
of acts.[35] He is led by his uncertainty to assume the guilty act.
Rendered mad by this assumption, he wants only to prove
that Desdemona is unfaithful. He still regards himself as the
dispenser of justice. But now it is no longer the health of the
military order that supports his authority, but his right to be
loved. His need for her love has been converted into a duty
for her to love, a duty which he takes it on himself to judge.
But a judge should have no interest in the one he judges. As
his doubt has grown, his whole way of life and manner of understanding have changed. He is no longer free and open of
manner or trusting of disposition. He is suspicious. Acts no
longer mean to Othello what they seem to mean. Decent appearances now conceal an underlying viciousness, and this
viciousness can be said to be physical passion. Chastity has
become a cult with him.[36] Desdemona's free offer of a chaste

love, which was so unexpected and which he accepted as his due, he now insists upon. Now, however, he believes this offer to be unnatural. Men are naturally lustful beasts; chastity without compulsion becomes unintelligible to him. Desdemona must be sequestered from society and compelled to spend her life in prayer if she is to be purged of the appetites that make her unworthy of Othello.[37] On the basis of his need, he wishes to force men counter to their natures; what was supposed to be love now turns into a tyranny. With it comes a peculiarly low view of mankind.

Iago becomes the high priest of this cult, leading Othello "by the nose." Iago converts all men into obscene beasts in Othello's eyes. He shows Othello that the love and honor due him is destroyed by physical passion; human beings are naturally led to care for things of the flesh. In order to be believed in, Othello must change this; his jealousy, under Iago's guidance, becomes a demand for inhuman purity, for a renunciation of the worship of the body. Iago has only to suggest obscene motivations and Othello is ready to wreak vengeance on any who are suspected. Iago makes use of an intense hate and fear of lust on Othello's part to further his own ends. Iago becomes a moralizer on the very basis of his lewd preoccupations. His moralizing reaches its almost comic peak when he comments on Cassio's fate—"This is the fruit of whoring." [38] He is a priest who makes use of Othello's new morality to conceal his private ends. I know of no play within which physical passion is believed to be so much the source of the action and, in reality, is so little the source of any important thing. More subtle vices of the soul are the roots of the action.

The new attempt to control souls leads of necessity to a new method of understanding men. Souls cannot be seen. Of course, a justice which saw men's souls naked would be vastly superior to the old justice, in which judgment was rendered only on the basis of acts committed. But perhaps the old way was founded on a prudent reserve, or modesty, which recognized the limitations of human vision. The result of the new way is not to truly see the soul, but rather to reject all the evidence of action and to turn to signs which in themselves have no meaning. Desdemona is judged by the handkerchief, that handkerchief on which the whole judgment turns. It is a magic charm, of superhuman quality, and only through it can she control Othello.[39] When she does not appear to show sufficient respect for this object, this mere thing, she is guilty, and her soul is laid bare. Mere routine or ritual is the basis of the judgment of Desdemona. The attempt to do away with the superficiality of the old law leads to a mysticism which is even more distant from truth.

Othello commits his terrible crime for the sake of justice. The horror of the murder only reflects the fact that justice must be stern. If Othello is right about Desdemona's deed and is further correct in assuming that her only salvation would be in loving him, then his cruelty would be but terrible responsibility. He may justly say that "I who am cruel, am yet merciful." [40] Mercy can appear in this gruesome context because Othello's bloodiness is an integral part of the human scene in the new context created by him, and any attempt to soften the lot of those under his sovereignty can be regarded as mercy. On the basis of the new justice of love, a cruelty and passion that never before existed comes into being.

V

Othello sought to accomplish an extreme human feat; he attempted to be a hero without a home, without a city to sing his praises and write his epitaph. He did this under the guise of universality; only if a man is liberated from the influence of and need for the laws and ways of a particular nation can he go anywhere and be a hero. But this universality, Shakespeare seems to tell us, is a lie. If a man can liberate himself from a particular time and place, it cannot be as a hero, statesman, or soldier. Such careers are by their nature bound to the fortunes of cities of men, all of which have special needs and traditions. Those who follow these paths seek glory as their reward, and glory is dependent on a public. The hero is perforce attached to the place whence his glory comes, and he must believe somehow in the special importance and excellence of that place. This represents a denial of the universal standpoint; it is part of the necessary narrowing of the statesman's horizon.

Othello's universality only conceals a desire to be limited

and local; it is itself an inflated shadow of the ordinary man's limitations; it is his tool for entry into Venice. Man's eternal aspiration to be man and man alone is burlesqued and travestied; what should be truly an end in itself and masquerades as such is but a means in Othello's usage. He pretends to be lovable because he is good, but actually his goodness is only an appearance to enable him to be loved. As long as he believes his own myth, he can be gentle, for he thinks that what he demands from men is natural. But, when he comes to doubt, he believes that what he demands is against nature. His jealousy then becomes his weapon to bend men to his will. His barbaric nature now reveals itself; but it is barbarism transformed and intensified.

His final tragedy consists, not so much in killing Desdemona, but in the discovery of his own injustice—that his justice is not justice at all. He discovers that what he thought was justice was but a way of gratifying his own appetite, an appetite whose existence it was of the essence of his being not to recognize. His jealousy arises when he realizes that he is a dependent being, that he needs. His tragedy is complete when it becomes clear that he does not deserve fulfillment, but only desires it. He has done terrible deeds under the conviction of his own wisdom, but he is nothing. Othello is a figure of enormous proportions; no reader can fail to sense this. Yet he is curiously insubstantial. And this is Shakespeare's meaning: he is a name without a substance. He lives in men's minds and needs more than in any reality. Both for his own sake and for that of the Venetians, he had to be thought a perfect being, but he was only a being afflicted with human passion. The intensity of the ending comes from the loud bursting of an enormous bubble which vanishes into nothingness.[41] His last words protest his everlasting loyalty to Venice.

Shakespeare appears to tell us that it is not good to introduce influences that are too foreign, regardless of the guise in which they may come. The benevolence of foreign influences is always ambiguous. What is not native will at some point go against the grain of what is native; it must then tyrannize or succumb. Venice did not suffer from it, but Desdemona did; Venice knew when to "cast him." Universality on the purely political level does not conduce to the city's good.

VI

Let us turn now to Desdemona. Her selfless devotion to Othello and her sweetness make her a peculiarly undeserving subject for tragic suffering. Her death seems deeply offensive. It must be asked whether there is anything in her nature that makes her fate in any way appropriate. Is she senselessly destroyed, a harmless bystander caught in the backlash of the unreeling of Othello's life?

The answer is dependent on an understanding of her love. What was the source of her involvement in this strange romance? The absolute source was Othello's speeches. But this is not enough in itself; we must discover to what these speeches appealed. We learn from her father that she was ordinarily a quiet and shy girl, a soft and gentle character. But, at the same time, we know that she was independent, that she knew her own wishes. She had "shunned the wealthy curled darlings" of Venice; she was not satisfied with the best of Venice.[42] She wanted to love something beyond the Venetian.

This, Othello provided. His stories of strange lands and great adventures seemed to give evidence of an experience and knowledge beyond the conventional. She felt that her limited life was not sufficient; we see in her an embryonic passion for the universal, a desire not to be duped by life. But she is undirected. What is merely different and strange impresses her as more significant and real. Whether Othello believes them or not, his stories contain much that could not possibly be true; they are, as Iago says, fantastic.[43] They appeal to Desdemona's imagination, which was watered with loneliness and shyness. She is exactly as her name describes her—superstitious.[44] Her devotion to Othello exalts her, and her choice to seek for meaning beyond accepted belief lends her a dignity which the ordinary citizen cannot have. But it was a choice conceived in error; Othello was a creation of her mind. She believed his speeches about his deeds. Paradoxically, her love sought in Othello something independent and free, while that very love made him dependent and bound his seeming universality to something particular. They passed each other by, as it were, on the path of love. Most paradoxical of all, in order to free herself from Venice, she loved a creation of Venice. Instead of winning her freedom, she became all the more fettered to the thing she was trying to escape; Othello existed only in the mind of Venice. Desdemona gave herself completely and with passion to something beyond the physical, but to a something conceived in error. In giving up all for the sake of cosmopolitanism, she was a follower of the most characteristic expression of the political community—its myths about its leaders. Desdemona, the only figure in the play who is indifferent to popular opinion, becomes a prisoner of the opinion about Othello.

Desdemona's superstition is not the only cause of her death. Her fidelity is also a necessary condition. She was not only attracted by Othello's stories, but she believed and insisted on keeping faith with him no matter what he did. The appearance of his actions is unimportant; he must be followed and loved regardless of his deeds, for his ends are inscrutable. She believes in him so completely that she must deny the validity of common sense in order to justify him. What appears as injustice from an ordinary point of view must appear to Desdemona as justice punishing some supposed vice or sin in herself or others. If he is to be believed in, although he acts contrary to ordinary human standards, then she must say that those standards are meaningless or are misconceived in this higher context. She accepts that new way of judging souls that resulted from Othello's jealousy; the clear appearance of things is rejected, and some mysterious standard dependent on Othello's whim becomes the rule. Of course, the real source of this standard is Othello's need to make himself loved absolutely and uncontingently. But that true source is transformed and represented as a hidden meaning to life, one that can be revealed only through Othello. In Desdemona, there begins a sort of self-examination; no longer does she look to the surface meaning of words and deeds, but her conscience bids her to search out faults which her reason does not see. Cassio did much the same thing when dismissed by Othello; all moral value comes from Othello, and what he does not approve is bad. Othello does not depend on nature, but nature on Othello. This leads to new habits of mind, new virtues.

Desdemona, in her conversation with Emilia, states her principle clearly: fidelity and only fidelity—everything subordinated to it. It is noble, without doubt, but it certainly is not so reasonable as the statement of Emilia, who makes fidelity dependent on the deeds of the husband. Her morality is an easy-going one that does not attach so much significance to chastity. In herself, she is not so fine a person as Desdemona, but perhaps true and untragic nobility cannot be reached by the sanctification of marital fidelity. Emilia, for all her inferiority, may yet serve to point this out. For Emilia, the simple world of common-sense meanings and the evident justice of acts must dictate to fidelity; fidelity cannot be unconditional. For Desdemona, everything must be interpreted in such a way as to preserve her faith.[45]

Desdemona's faith in Othello leads her to a certain disregard for the truth which has not been often enough observed. We see her practicing deception three times in the play, and each time with great significance for her fate. In the first place, she hides her relationship with Othello from her father and presents him with the *fait accompli*. However indulgently we may look on her love for Othello, there is no question but that she is guilty of disobedience, and her love comes into conflict with most sacred duties. The love of Othello leads the best of the city's children to a contempt for it and a willingness to break the law for his sake. In any case of conflict of loyalties, Desdemona chooses without hesitation in favor of Othello; it seems that this shy girl gained so much strength and confidence or such fanaticism from her love that she is capable of doing things in a cool spirit that others would be unable to do. It must be remembered that the consequence of this deception was the death of her father.[46] In the second case, she lied to Othello about the handkerchief. Here is perhaps the clearest indication of her superstitious nature; she was so frightened by the significance Othello attached to the handkerchief and the tale he told her about it that she did not dare to let him know that she had lost it. This untruth led directly to her own death.[47] Finally, she seems to tell a lie even after death. She says that

Othello did not kill her. She still tries to preserve his reputation; for she would die in vain if he were evil. His reputation lives in her and not in him. To the end, she must see things as she wants them to be rather than as they are. Believing is seeing.[48]

Desdemona's death is in large measure due to her own errors. They were noble errors, errors which elevated her above the level of ordinary humanity, but they deserved punishment. From the point of view of everyday life, Desdemona sins in deceiving her father. We take her side because she does so in the name of something higher. But perhaps, from a third and highest standpoint, we must come to the defense of civil society and see her defection as a result of a monstrous misconception. Perhaps the true cosmopolitanism can be attained only by renouncing the dearest hopes of practical life. Marriage is a part of political life, of civil society. One cannot purify it of its political element without depriving it of its substance.

Desdemona has been compared to Cordelia and Miranda, and with much justice. She is independent, courageous, and gentle, as is the former, and she has a sweet ingenuousness like the latter (in the spirit of "oh, brave new world"). But Desdemona lacks that love of the truth which causes Cordelia to understand her situation so well. Desdemona never recognizes her error, and, using the other possible meaning of her name, she says, "It is my wretched fortune." [49] Shakespeare, in the fullness of his meaning, says that her "wretched fortune" is a result of her "superstition." Unlike Miranda, she has no Prospero to guide her imagination and set her on the right course. Her untutored understanding spawns monsters. Shakespeare in this bleak play shows us no way around Desdemona's problem. She leads a noble life, but one that is against law and against reason.

VII

Finally, let us consider the last member of the play's trinity, Iago. Iago is clearly the Devil. He says so himself and is often so called.[50] But, in the case where God is not perfect, the Devil's negativity may be a source of liberation, an aid to the discovery of the truth. Iago has always been condemned and hated, and certainly what he does is most terrible; but a defense can and must be made for him.[51] Shakespeare plays on a human softness and sentimentality in this work. We so like to flatter our own goodness and warmheartedness that we are unwilling to recognize hard truths. Our natural partisanship with love and lovers causes us to see only Iago's wickedness in destroying the love of Othello and Desdemona; we like to believe that, without his intervention, all would have been well. But the very terribleness which so moves us teaches us, albeit unconsciously, that this is not just another love story, that there is here an inevitability we wish not to face, one we hide in our condemnation of Iago.

Iago, as I have said, is only a mirror or an agent that causes the unseen to become visible. Lived over and over again, the love of Desdemona and Othello would end the same way. Yet, no matter how often it happened, each time we would be as shocked and surprised as we were the first time, for the result runs counter to our wish, and our wishes cause us to bury the truth. Shakespeare is, in the final accounting, very hard. Iago's speeches, read dispassionately, show that he is the clearest thinker in the play. "Honest Iago" is not merely a tragically misplaced epithet. Iago does tell more of the truth than any other character. It is difficult to understand his motivation; no villain in Shakespeare seems to act without some plausible end in view, an end the value of which all men would recognize, though they might perhaps not be willing to commit the crimes necessary to arrive at it. But Iago, as does the Devil, seems to act from pure negativity. I am not what I am.[52] Whatever Othello wants, Iago wants the opposite. He is sub- or superhuman. But, in opposing Othello, he shows that the world dominated by Othello is a world of fancy. He speaks out for a freedom which none of the others recognize. Iago wishes to live his own life free from the domination of other men, and especially of other men's thoughts. He realizes that true tyranny is not imposed by force, but imposes itself on the minds of men. For Iago, man can free himself only by thought. He has thought through the emptiness of most beliefs and will not live in subordination to them. He cannot found his life on self-deception, as Othello does.[53]

His analysis of things generally esteemed leads to several conclusions. He is, in the first place, a materialist. The solidity of money as a means of living freely is clear, so he does not share the noble man's contempt for it. (The noble man usually has money already, so is not forced to the salutary reflection on its necessity.) The word "purse" is often found in his mouth. In the second place, he knows that reputation is often ill gained and worse lost. He not only knows it but demonstrates it in his manipulations of Othello and Cassio and by his own very good repute. A man must be independent of reputation, or he is the slave of public whim. He tells this beautifully to Cassio, and, to show how opposite Othello's view is, Iago tells him that reputation is everything and the purse trash. For Iago, reputation is trash, and he who follows it lives for others. Since reputation is no real sign of true virtue, it follows that straightforward honesty is undesirable. A man must appear to be what the public wants, and freedom to live well depends on cultivating deception.

Iago reveals the strange fact that freedom to pursue the truth requires deception, for the truth runs counter to much necessary prejudice; he who wants to be open must either be a martyr or deceive himself for the sake of popularity. Moreover, Iago is the only character who has comic lines in an unusually humorless play. The serious things, so piously considered by the others, are subjects of his wit. Part of his freedom comes from being able to laugh at mankind, to see that much of its pretension is comic. Connected with this is his contempt for romantic love. He sees nothing in it beyond physical passion. Love cannot take on such grand significance for him, and the attempt to make it sacred is ridiculous.[54]

All the bonds that link humanity and make living together possible have been dissolved in Iago. Trust is impossible for him because to trust implies respect for other human beings, a respect in which he is completely deficient.[55] When a man believes that public opinion or his own sense of shame are merely devices of the herd to make men live for others rather than for themselves, all the monsters of passion are released within him. Iago is jealous, lecherous, and ambitious; his reason and reasonableness allow him to divest himself of all the clogs of convention, but give him no stable goals for action. Only his emancipated passions supply him with objects of desire. Iago himself has no idea of what he wants. He is eminently a private man; he can care for no one but himself, and his views justify this selfishness, for there is no reason to serve a morality created in the interest of others.[56] He is an example of what is often asserted will happen when men no longer believe in God; he is an atheist.

If such a private view of life and man is grafted onto the thought of a political man, a man who is interested in public life, the result is the development of a severe, punishing morality. A political man knows of the necessity of civil society, that the common good can only be served if there is a habit of obedience to law and a deference to custom. If he is convinced that men are by nature bad, then he must believe in the use of force, deceit, and terror to make them conform. Iago succeeds in convincing Othello of his own view of mankind, yet this does not alter Othello's way of life; he does not renounce public life and vow to pursue his own passions, as would seem reasonable for a man with such an opinion. He decides instead to force men to be what he formerly thought they naturally were. Othello was peculiarly susceptible to this persuasion, for he was not a member of a city where men through long habit have learned to live together and where they do not indulge themselves in questioning whether it is good or not that they do so. Even if they raised the question, the force of habit would be likely to keep them in their civil ways.

Othello, on the other hand, cannot rest content with obedience grounded on unconscious repetition; he is universal and a stranger and requires that man deliberately choose the good. It is perhaps true that the majority of men, outside the particular training which has broken them to their city's laws, would not be so just and would be more likely to consult their private interests. Othello is gentle and loving as long as he believes in man's goodness; he becomes a tyrant when he doubts. To fit the cosmopolis of which he dreams, men must be transformed, and what was once innocuous in them now becomes a great danger. Iago wants and needs the change he produces in Othello. He does not believe in the common good. But, when he can control Othello and use Othello's fears to punish others, he will be in a perfect position to do as he lists. His apparently unmotivated vengeance expresses his freedom. A morality based on ritual and suspicion fits the needs of this hypocrite, informer, and false accuser. Tartuffes can always stand for morality. The Devil can quote scripture, especially when he has written it. Iago makes use of Othello's good but misguided intentions, and Othello's tragedy comes when he realizes that his life has been used to destroy others for the sake of an Iago. Iago is Othello's ensign, or standard-bearer, in something more than name.

Iago is also an outsider in Venice; he is not of the senatorial class and may even be a foreigner; he need not practice self-deception, since he does not care for honor. For him, his profession is simply a job. He has no need to try to add dignity to it, hence he is not compelled to try to make Venice's beliefs his own. Of course, the result of this is that he cannot participate in the heroic character of an Othello. However revealing his existence may be—and the truth is not an unimportant thing—his is not a life that men would wish to imitate. His critique of ordinary beliefs leaves him in the end with no real purpose in life at all. He opposes established custom in the name of freedom, but this freedom is compatible with the basest and most arbitrary ends. He can trust no one and is full of fear that he himself will be deceived because men are base. His negativity leads only to the breakdown of order and turns his life into a chaos.

Othello appears, then, to leave us with this choice—a mean life based on a clear perception of reality or a noble life based on falsehood and ending in tragedy. Othello is open and loving, but deceived. Iago knows well the defects of Othello's life, but certainly offers no alternative worthy of choice. Yet Iago, in the end, is himself destroyed, but not by the baseness he understands and fears. Iago, otherwise so clear-sighted, fails to see one thing. He cannot foresee that Emilia would be willing to die for the truth. The possibility of a simple, unadorned passion for nothing but truth is not within his ken. But would not a life expressing such a passion be both noble and, by its very nature, free of deception?

N O T E S

1 *Characteristicks* (London: 1727), Vol. I, pp. 347-350.

2 For this reason, Iago is never able to work directly on Desdemona; if she has vices, they are not of the self-interested variety. He has no way of acting on her, no lever with which to move her. Iago can only influence those around Desdemona and hence accomplish her disaster.

3 I. i. 78. All citations are to the Furness variorum edition (Philadelphia: J. B. Lippincott Co., 1886).

4 I. i. 118; cp. 86-88; I. ii. 13-19.

5 I. ii. 78-98; cp. I. iii. 75-79.

6 I. iii. 115-117; cp. II. i. 262-263; III. iii. 270-274.

7 Cf. A. C. Bradley, *Shakespearean Tragedy* (London: 1929), pp. 198-203. In addition to Bradley's excellent reasonings, it may be mentioned that Aaron the Moor in *Titus Adronicus* is black and that the Prince of Morocco in the *Merchant of Venice* is apparently so (II. i. 1-16; II. vii. 81). In *Othello*, there are these references to his color: I. i. 72, 96-97, 116 (Barbary horses were black); ii. 87-88; iii. 320-321; II. ii. 48; III. iii. 308. "Black" clearly does not mean "Moorish" as we understand it, but simply "black." Shakespeare had a definite dramatic purpose in making Othello as black as possible and could rely on the convention of the theater and the inexperience of the audience to permit this alteration of reality.

8 Cf. I. i. 105-153; I. ii. 78-98; I. iii. 75-79; II. i. 254-270.

9 Cf. *Merchant of Venice* II. ii, vii; *Othello* I. i. 16-18; II. i. 255-256. The Prince of Morocco speaks of war and his own heroism; he has a high-flown and dramatic manner of speech different from that of the other characters; he tells of his high birth and uses it as a justification for his suit; and he, too, seems sincerely attached to the beautiful Venetian.

10 The fact that Othello mentions his own high lineage (I. ii. 22-27) can well mean that he feels he must do so. He protests the fact. It is probable that his royal birth was not recognized at Venice and, if it was, nevertheless was not considered to constitute equality with Venetian nobility. Even if Othello is himself really persuaded that he comes from stock as good as that into which he has married, Brabantio does not accept it as such.

11 I. iii. 290-293; cf. Furness' excellent note, pp. 75-76; III. iii. 309-310.

12 Cf. Desdemona's "I saw Othello's visage in his mind"—I. iii. 280; cp. Note 8.

13 This is a possibility hinted at by both Iago and the duke and somewhat supported by Othello's judicious choice of the moment of marriage, when he was most needed; I. ii. 60-61; iii. 195, 252 ff.; cp. I. i. 162-168. Both charges—that Othello used drugs and that he was a fortune-hunter—are in some measure justified by the event, although not in the vulgar way intended by their authors. He did bewitch Desdemona by his stories more powerful than any drug, and he was seeking a place in the world.

14 I. i. 162-168.

15 This is precisely what Shaftesbury objects to. He sees Othello as a talker and not a doer. He impresses Desdemona with lies (cp. Iago, II. i. 255-257) and touches her naïve fantasy. Such stories are a great danger, and even the Bible, because of its strangeness, is not, according to Shaftesbury, a suitable source for the stories of poets. The proper subjects with which to impress the young are those that are probable and within the compass of reason. Only pretenders who wish to overwhelm and cause suspension of the critical faculties behave as does Othello. Shaftesbury apparently believes that such stories as those of "men whose heads do grow beneath their shoulders" were evident falsehoods and meant by Shakespeare to be understood as such.

16 That a city is not something that one can just choose is clearly Shakespeare's view; one need only consider the political settings of the various plays, and especially those of the historical works. There are differing national characters, and the kind of action which is typical varies from place to place; the plays situated in ancient Rome are certainly very different in men and interest from those that take place in modern Venice or Verona. Long tradition, stock, climate, and laws change everything. There are very few plays of Shakespeare which could be imagined as taking the same course in another locale. *Titus Andronicus* is in a way a drama concerning a man born out of his time, if not place; and much of the often-remarked absurdity of the piece comes from the fact of Titus Andronicus' attempt to act like an old Roman gentleman among barbarians. Not many heroes in Shakespeare could easily be transferred in time or place and still retain the decisive aspects of their characters or still deal with the same problems; Prospero is perhaps one. But simple cosmopolitanism, from the Shakespearean standpoint, would rob men of all that is interesting in them, bringing about a unity at the lowest common denominator. Dramatically speaking, at least, most great men are great because they are devoted to the highest goals of a particular political entity which has chosen, willfully or no, to develop one aspect of the human possibility at the sacrifice of others. Old Romans cannot live as modern Danes do, and, if one attempted to combine the two, the deepest features of both would be lost. To participate in a particular political community depends on birth and education, on accidents.

17 This to prove that he should be treated well by Venetians. Cf. Note 10.

18 Precisely what he has done for Venice, we do not learn. But that he has a great repute as a leader is made clear enough; I. iii. 249-252; IV. i. 295-296.

19 This question evidently preoccupied Shakespeare very much, for he treats it again, in another way, in *Coriolanus*. This is the case of a man much at home in Rome but who resents his dependence on what he considers the vulgar mass; he wants to be free of what created him. In attempting to liberate himself, he loses his soul. The problem is again to what extent the hero is free of those who acclaim him. Coriolanus is very conscious of the problem, whereas Othello is not;

this is why the former leaves Rome and the latter can stay in Venice.

[20] II. ii. 194-196; V. ii. 427-429; II. ii. 373-375; V. ii. 36-37. Brabantio calls him a pagan; I. ii. 121.

[21] I. i. 162-168. The duke asks after a certain Marcus Luccicos, who, as it turns out, is not in Venice; he sends after Marcus in the same terms in which he sent after Othello; I. iii. 52-56; cp. I. ii. 43-45.

[22] Othello's victory over Brabantio in the hearing before the duke is a good model of the strengths and weaknesses of his situation. The moment at which Brabantio must make his plea is a troubled and confused one; the state is endangered, and foreign threats cause Othello to be needed. When they enter together, the confident Brabantio (I. ii. 115-121) is completely ignored by the suave duke, who looks to Othello immediately (I. iii. 60ff.). The justice of the case is evidently not so much to be considered as the current crisis and the fact that Othello is indispensable in it. The ordinary order of respect and indulgence is temporarily abridged. The duke is polite to Brabantio (it is questionable how much Brabantio's person—as opposed to his position, wealth, and family—was actually respected in the city, for he had not been called to the council, and he was to have been found at home); when he hears Brabantio's complaint, he promises all support before he finds out who is responsible. As soon as he hears Othello's name, he changes his tone and gives Othello every chance to defend himself. One can well wonder how the duke would have behaved in other conditions and whether he would then have permitted such a marriage without the father's consent or allowed a foreigner such rights in the city. At all events, he supports Othello while trying to assuage Brabantio. He moralizes with the embittered Brabantio, who justly responds that it is easy for one who is unhurt to give sympathy. The duke is a subtle statesman; he attempts to give the appearance of perfect morality while keeping his eye on the expedient. Shakespeare expresses this beautifully by putting the duke's moralizing into rhyming verse. Afterward, he reverts to ordinary prose as soon as he is able to treat the serious business at hand.

He gets over with rhetoric what is for him the very inconvenient and unpleasant affair of Desdemona's marriage to return to the important consideration, which has really determined his decision, and real business is prosaic (I. iii. 225-254). But Othello's advantage in a crisis disappears with his very success. In the first lines of the play, Iago irritates Roderigo's civic pride by presenting Othello as a foreigner lording it over the native nobility (I. i. 12-14). The prejudice is always lying in wait for the moment when no compelling reasons demand its repression. Cf. I. i. 138-139, 148-158. Brabantio remains in Venice and is still a force to be reckoned with. The anger of Brabantio can make the duke uncomfortable, for Brabantio is always in Venice and is independent of any appointment or crisis; Othello can be sent away and forgotten with no inconvenience to anyone if there is no external danger to the state. Perhaps Othello's recall was Brabantio's doing? At least this is what Desdemona guesses that Othello suspects (IV. ii. 53-56).

23 Cf. Note 18.

24 II. ii. 291-305. Iago can well appreciate the ambiguous character of reputation, for he enjoys a good one himself. But, when Iago speaks to Othello, he does so as though there were nothing questionable in reputation (III. iii. 181-188). He knows his man. A noble man never does anything that is considered shameful, and the opinion of his fellows is the guarantee of his own goodness. A man who cares about his reputation is likely to perform acts of a nature to gain it; the man who consults only his private inclinations is likely to be base. But, if reputation is a fickle thing, then the whole orientation of the gentleman or the proud man is placed in doubt. The perfect disciple of Othello is Cassio. He believes completely in Othello; this is the source of his unquestioning devotion and makes him a good lieutenant. But, from what he suffers and the undeserving way he loses his reputation, the lesson would seem to be that it is folly to live for the sake of others who do not understand and are acting from their own passions. Cassio expresses what his faith in Othello means when he says that reputation is the immortal part of himself (II. ii. 291-292; cp. 117-135; Romans 9:18; 8:24).

25 I. iii. 190-191; III. iii. 218.

26 Plato *Symposium* 189ᶜ-193ᵉ, 199ᵈ-204ᶜ; the *Lysis;* Aristotle *Metaphysics* XII. vii. 4; Cervantes *Don Quixote* I. xiv. This is so even in the highest sort of love—the good man who admires another good man because he sees his own virtues mirrored in the other and can honor them as he could not his own. Such love is based on the need for mutual admiration and a completion of one's own imperfect virtues. Cf. Aristotle *Nichomachean Ethics* IX. ix.

27 II. ii. 376-379. Shakespeare vividly depicts Othello's first consciousness of the depth and intensity of his need when, after Iago's first, tentative barbs, Desdemona arrives to plead for Cassio. He for the first time is a little vexed; all is not perfect as formerly, but, as she goes away, he cannot help admiring her and says, "Excellent wretch!" (III. iii. 104-106). He sees, with a certain pleasure, that he needs her very much and that it is somewhat in spite of himself, that it has nothing to do with right or justice. A few moments later, when his suspicions become explicit, he denies this and says that he would let her go if she were false; he soon realizes that, whatever she be, he must possess her or kill her, that he cannot do without her.

28 The importance of Desdemona to Othello as a tribute is clear when his rage against her reaches its height at the moment he is recalled by Venice. The crude impression which those who witness it have—that he is disturbed by losing his position—is not totally unjustified, with the qualification that we understand the deep sense in which his position is meaningful to him. He is ambitious, but in no vulgar way (IV. i. 231-317).

29 III. iii. 158-160.

30 III. iii. 455-456, 471-486, 499-501. By the beginning of Act IV, the discussion of the meaning of physical acts has turned into a gruesome and tantalizing game (IV. i. 1-26). The obscenity of Iago is founded on that which is revered by others. For both Brabantio and Othello,

the purity of Desdemona is all in all. The shocking aspect of Iago's speech is not that he speaks freely about sensual matters, but that for others these things are sacred and that Iago profanes what is holy for them. It is only in the context of reverence that Iago's speech is terrible; it is a sort of blasphemy. The relation between Othello and Desdemona, if there is any physical element to it at all, is largely a spiritual one. When he realizes that perhaps physical satisfactions are important for her and he sees his own insufficiency in this regard, her possible infidelity becomes all the more horrible for him. It is not only that she cares for another, but that her being is so constituted that he could never satisfy her. He must insist on not only fidelity but chastity; he must change her nature and all men's natures, and all this, not for the sake of morality, but to preserve for himself that which he wants.

31 God's jealousy in relation to Israel in the Old Testament is interpreted in parable as the relation of a man to a faithless woman (Ezekiel 16:38), and, in general, the action of God is understood in analogy to the conduct of husbands. Because of the sanctity of marriage, the husband's care gains greater justice, and, because of the holiness of the husband's jealousy, the analogy of God's jealousy to that of man is not obnoxious. Jealousy, the emotion accompanying the *suspicion* of infidelity, is not an important theme outside the Biblical tradition. "Ein Beleg für die Bdtg. Eifersucht speziell im Verhältniss von Ehegatten ist mir im klass. Griech. nicht begegnet" (A. Stumpf, in Kittel's *Theologische Wörterbuch zum Neuen Testament* [Stuttgart: 1935], p. 879). No treatment of the subject can be found in Greek literature on the passions. At the least, it can be said that fidelity to, and love of, God take on a new and special sense when it is understood that God commands them because he is jealous. The magnitude of Othello's jealousy, in both its understanding of marriage and its *imitatio Dei*, is inconceivable without the Bible.

Shakespeare draws out the parallel in presenting the relationship between Othello and Desdemona as spiritual, with the physical motivations appearing as the great sin. Immediately before declaring his jealousy, the God of the Old Testament specifies the meaning of infidelity: the worship of physical objects—all that paganism implied (Exodus 20:4-6; cp. IV. i. 137).

32 II. ii. 232-234; III. iii. 417-419; V. ii. 110, 57 (cp. Mark 4:39), 165 (cp. Deut. 22:21), 167 (cp. Gen. 49:4). Othello's arrogation of godlike prerogatives is clearest in the assurance with which he judges—prior to his jealousy, in a calm confidence in his superiority to others, later, in the righteous intensity of his fury. When he learns that he was in error, he is nothing—he is either perfection or nothingness.

33 III. iii. 205-221.

34 II. ii. 229-234, 288-292.

35 Othello does indeed begin by demanding deeds—ocular proof, as was his custom. He does not want to be led by simple sentiments; he wants to do justice. But Iago skillfully shows him that, in such matters, direct proof is impossible, and Othello is satisfied with ritual

proofs turned into "confirmations strong as proofs of holy writ" (III. iii. 375-377) by the mad assurance that all men are base and inclined to acts of treachery; jealousy presupposes guilt and seeks substantiation (III. iii. 219-221, 415-514).

36 III. iii. 312-314; III. iv. 46-52; IV. i. 9-12; ii. 24-27. At the end, even the stars are the signs of a cosmic chastity; V. ii. 4.

37 III. iv. 43-56.

38 Iago's use of morality is fully conscious and is based on his observation of Othello. Actually, the attitude he takes is much nearer that of those who are attached to Othello than to his own natural one. Cassio, when dismissed by Othello, speaks in terms worthy of the most severe moralist, "the devil wine, the devil anger," etc. In talking to him, Iago takes a reasonable and tolerant line (II. ii. 292-343). Cassio orients himself according to the pleasure and displeasure of Othello and, in his fall from grace, blames himself with extraordinary severity; rather than trying to re-establish himself, he falls into a state of repentance and self-castigation. Desdemona is much the same way. Both torment only themselves, and Iago sees where this attitude can lead if made cynical use of. If those who love Othello are dependent on his opinion and he is jealous and frightened of losing their love, Iago, by playing on Othello's fear, can cause him to make more and more demands on others and so further his own ends (e.g., his suggestion that fear is the best way to control Desdemona; III. iii. 236-238). All he need do is present Othello with new dangers, and his standards become ever higher and sterner. Othello's sick fears convert innocent human acts into crimes. The height of the morality comes only from Iago's low view of men. Cassio's harmless weakness at drink and his love for women can in this context be converted into mortal sins. It is interesting to note that Othello's tyranny is prefigured by Brabantio's reaction on recognizing that he is deceived; I. iii. 221-224.

39 III. iv. 68-81. Shakespeare has taken the handkerchief—a much less significant element in the source, Cinthio's *novella*—and rendered it a magic charm in which the whole proof of Othello's suspicions is centered and fulfilled. It is the sole and sufficient cause of Desdemona's death.

40 V. ii. 110.

41 V. ii. 304-307; cp. III. iii. 403-413.

42 I. iii. 113-115; I. ii. 83.

43 I. iii. 166-168; II. i. 255-257.

44 In this etymology, I follow Shaftesbury in considering it to be derived from the Greek δεισιδαίμων, whereas the later interpreters have unanimously understood it as stemming from δυσδαίμων, meaning "ill-starred" or "ill-fated." One cannot, of course, lean too heavily on the supposed etymology of a name in the interpretation of a play, especially when that etymology is itself disputable. But it seems certain that Shakespeare often chose names which had an overtone of their bearer's character (cf. Ruskin, *Munera Pulveris*, in *Works* [London: 1905], p. 257), and in this case both meanings would apply extremely well. My preference for the meaning "superstitious"

72

is grounded on a general observation of her nature and the suitability of applying such a term to her. As far as I am able to see, there are no philological grounds for the preference of the one interpretation over the other, so that one must rely on one's interpretation of the play to justify the sense of the name. If the interpretation is convincing, the name gives a certain added weight. The other interpreters who have treated this problem have based their choice almost exclusively on a belief that Desdemona was unlucky and that this constitutes her essence; the meaning of her name is only an expression of this. The burden of this essay has been to prove that it is not simply ill fortune that constitutes the core of her tragedy. The reader must himself judge the plausibility of the two etymologies, because scholarship can go no further. As is frequent in scholarly matters, an assumption as to the certitude of a questionable interpretation seems to provide scientific proof of issues really contingent on that interpretation. Only if a Shaftesbury is certainly wrong in his understanding of *Othello* can it be definitely decided that "ill-starred" is what was meant by Shakespeare.

Whatever confirming evidence there is is ambiguous. Shakespeare's source, Cinthio, contained only this one name which was taken over by Shakespeare. In Cinthio, the name almost certainly means "ill-starred"; but this does not prove that Shakespeare could not have altered this just as he reinterprets the entire character and gives it a new significance. One relevant fact is that Shakespeare alters Cinthio's spelling of the name; in the *novella*, it is "*Disdemona.*" The *i* or *y* are the conventional transliterations of the Greek *v*, which would clearly seem to mean that the etymology is δυσδαίμων. Shakespeare's substitution of *e* for *i*, if it is not for reasons of euphony which are not evident, would render the name closer to δεισιδαίμων. From Theophrastus, if not earlier, on down, the δεισιδαίμων, or superstitious man, is one of the conventional human types, a character that is painted in literature for the sake of instructing audiences about common and dangerous errors. Plutarch wrote a treatise about it which could easily have been read by Shakespeare. In Plutarch's work, the superstitious man is contrasted to the atheist—presented as having contrary false opinions about the nature of the gods. The two characters, as outlined by Plutarch, have striking similarities to Desdemona and Iago.

Finally, the two derivations are not necessarily mutually exclusive (cf. p. 62, *supra*). Cf. John Upton, *Critical Observations on Shakespeare* (London: 1746), p. 288; John Wesley Hales, *Notes and Essays on Shakespeare* (London: 1884), p. 111; Albert Tesch, "Zum Namen Desdemona," *Germanisch-Romanische Monatsschrift*, XVII (1929), 578-588.

[45] IV. iii. 66-116, 24-26; ii. 81, 131-145, 177-193; III. iii. 89-96, 103; iv. 162-176.
[46] V. ii. 255-261.
[47] III. iv. 95-104.
[48] V. ii. 147-156. Othello has smothered Desdemona at Line 105 and is persuaded she is dead by Line 117. Whether Shakespeare meant

that she return to life or Othello was mistaken and she was not yet quite dead, Desdemona's words—coherent sentences uttered after strangulation—constitute a remarkable occurrence, outside the natural order of things. This difficulty has often been noted. I suggest that this last supreme effort of the poor creature was intended to give a supernatural impression to the audience and that attempts to rationalize it, by changing the manner of her death or otherwise, miss the meaning. Precisely because of the improbability of what she does do we know of the intensity of Desdemona's devotion and faith; she gives it a significance beyond the human in a play distinguished by its merely human context, one in which the cosmic reverberations characterizing Shakespeare's other great tragedies are absent. In the theater, especially that of Shakespeare, improbabilities are the devices for the expression of greater but unutterable probabilities.

49 IV. ii. 150.

50 I. i. 169, 121-122; iii. 427; II. ii. 310-312, 323-325, 381-382; III. iv. 50; V. ii. 351-352.

51 Macaulay made an able one, cited in the Furness variorum, pp. 412-413.

52 I. i. 71; cp. Exodus 3:14; cp. III. iii. 104-106.

53 I. iii. 350-390.

54 II. i. 119-191.

55 Othello, on the contrary, believed that men are fundamentally what they seem to be (III. iii. 139-151; cp. I. iii. 422-425). Iago has made the distinction between seeming and being, and everything he does is based on it. One must live for the real, which is radically different from the apparent, while seeming to be what one is not. He can use Othello because Othello cares so much about appearance and because, once he, too, has begun to distrust appearance, he believes in the possible reality of anything. Iago's, "I never found a man who knew how to love himself" (I. iii. 344-345), is the expression of the moral attitude that is the result of his views.

56 I. i. 45-70.

4

The Morality of the
Pagan Hero

✍ *JULIUS CAESAR** ࿖

> But [Caesar's] great prosperitie and good
> fortune that favored him all his life time,
> did continue afterwards in the revenge of
> his death, pursuing the murtherers both
> by sea and land, till they had not left a
> man more to be executed, of al them that
> were actors or counsellors in the conspir-
> acy of his death.[1]

Julius Caesar is the story of a man who became a god. Beyond his merely human achievements—the destruction of
the Republic and the establishment of a universal monarchy
—he was worshiped as a divinity, as were many of those
who inherited his name. His appearance ended forever the
age of human heroes. Caesar brought to fulfillment the end
implied in all heroic ambition; he proved himself the best of
all men. He had no competitor; he was benefactor without
being beneficiary. Finally, his spirit ruled Rome, conveyed
the sole title to legitimacy, and punished all offenders against
it. He was, in short, self-sufficient.

Shakespeare analyzes this greatest of political accomplishments—the enormity of the talent required to compass it

* The idea for this essay was originally given me by Leo Strauss, and a
statement of that idea is to be found in Harry V. Jaffa's *Crisis of the
House Divided* (New York: Doubleday, 1959), pp. 215-216.

75

and the ambiguity of its worth once brought into being. We never see this prodigy in action; we see him speak, and we see the shadow he casts over the world so that men act only in relation to him and the very heavens seem to reflect his image. A study of the lesser figures who surrounded Caesar is the only way to an understanding of the elements which made him what he was and enabled him to do what he did. And their presentation is so complex that, for many, it is even unclear whether the hero is Caesar or Brutus. But, whatever one's conclusion on that, no one can deny that Caesar or what he represents dominates everyone in the play and that we must begin by looking at Caesar and his Rome.

I

Goethe[2] to the contrary, Shakespeare's Romans are not Englishmen, but real Romans, a distinct kind of men, differing from modern men in the character of their passions and their goals. He cloaked them in a garb recognizable to his audience; otherwise they would not have listened. But the essential diversity emerges. This is not to say that modernity or the fall of antiquity have changed human nature, but rather that new objects have been provided for its interest and that a new education forms it. It is precisely because human nature has not changed that the past is of interest. What men once were, we can still be.

The Romans were the products of other laws and a different understanding of the first things. Shakespeare made an effort to reproduce them so that we could grasp something of the meaning and worth of their institutions and beliefs. His endeavor is one of the most difficult a historian or playwright can undertake; he must convey a plausible picture to an audience which is alien to the character and goals of his subjects and even unaware of its ignorance of them. He himself must understand those subjects, who are so distant from any original experience he could have. The rediscovery of the atmosphere of ancient Rome is akin to the rediscovery, made in the Renaissance, of the beauty of classical sculpture. That art depicted men of a grace and nobility quite alien to what Europeans had grown accustomed to. It was attractive and enigmatic; it seemed to offer an alternative notion of humanity. But to understand that alternative required an intense effort of sympathy and scholarship, for men were no longer aware of what the ancients saw in the world or of the passions which moved them. It is no easy thing to capture an awareness of what one is not.

This undertaking was, in a sense, what we call the Renaissance. Along with the art of antiquity, the political life of ancient Rome began to attract interest and admiration. Rome had not been utterly forgotten, but it had been seen through the perspective of the Church Fathers' polemics against it; Rome had become part of a particular tradition. It had to be recovered from under the layers of prejudice, and the magnitude of this accomplishment can be felt if one compares Augustine's Rome to Machiavelli's. But it was a quest enlivened by expectation of the discovery of a new world.

Shakespeare is a product and fulfillment of this movement of rediscovery. His Roman plays present us with the essential Rome, and in them he tried to re-create those elusive qualities that made the Romans what they were. Rome, however, no longer interests modern men as it did all but our most recent predecessors, perhaps because we no longer need its example or possibly because we have forgotten what it was. It is well, therefore, to remind ourselves what Rome must have meant to at least the educated among Shakespeare's audience, for this consciousness is what he could count on in developing the stories of his heroes.

In Shakespeare's day, the remnants of the Roman Empire were still alive, and it was still remembered that Britain itself had been a part of it. There were still Caesars ruling, as was the case until World War I. The only nations that were graced with the adjective "civilized" were within the confines of that empire. The principles of law were either Roman or derived from Roman law. Liberal education was largely education in the Roman tongue; the philosophy and poetry that were the permanent standards of excellence were Roman or had been transmitted by the Romans. More important, the models of political greatness, either for individuals or nations, were Roman.

Whether for good or ill, the Roman achievement was so stunning that it could not fail to impress men who were interested in establishing respectable political orders. This single city had conquered the world and produced a multitude of heroes in every age until the fall of the Republic. This merely external side of Rome is played on by Shakespeare in both *Julius Caesar* and *Antony and Cleopatra*. One is constantly aware that the stake in the struggle for domination is the whole world. The problems of the heroes take on commensurate proportions, and so do their talents. The wishes and dreams of every public or private man find an extreme satisfaction in the very contemplation of this spectacle and the opportunity for fantasy which it affords.

It is against this background that the Roman plays must be seen. Rome is, in a way, everything—the source and the end. Whatever Shakespeare's final judgment of Rome may have been or however great the potential superiority of England may have appeared to him, Rome possesses, in his treatment of it, an incomparable splendor and grandeur. The Romans were the greatest political people who ever existed. They differed greatly from Elizabethan Englishmen. It would be far beyond my powers to delineate what the essential differences are; only reflection on the plays themselves can suggest an answer. But, crudely speaking, one can say that the Romans lacked two things possessed by the Englishmen—a single ruler and a single god. The Romans were neither monarchists nor Christians, but republicans and pagans. This has corresponding effects on the individual Romans. They were solely of this world, and their motivations were almost totally political or erotic. Some believed in gods, but those gods had to do only with political success or failure and did not give indications of a new transcendent dimension to life beyond that provided by civil society. The heroes were unabashedly ambitious of glory; their attention was not distracted by other charms or myths. They were an extraordinary number of able men, none recognizing a master, each honed to a superb edge of emulation.

In *Julius Caesar*, Shakespeare has chosen to depict the greatest of these great men. Paradoxically, it is the greatest Roman of them all who destroyed the Republic which was the seed bed of great Romans. Out of the constant and all-absorbing competition for the rewards of citizenship, finally emerged a victor who could subdue all of his opponents. This was the decisive moment in Roman history, the culmination of the Republic and the threshold of the Empire. The end once achieved, there was nothing left to be done. *Antony and Cleopatra* reveals this. Octavius merely inherits the name of Caesar and thereby inherits the fruits of Caesar's accomplishments. And Octavius is no hero; he is a dry opportunist with the capacity for neither loving nor fighting. Julius Caesar has so skillfully done his work that nothing of the old world can work within the new. It is Antony, in all his decadence, who is the last hero. The elements of the heroic have gone out of balance in him; his spiritedness and his *eros* go in different directions. But to what heights each of these contradictory impulses carry him! He is alive; the force and range of his character win us; and we are unable to resist a sense of bitterness at his inevitable defeat before the humanly inferior Octavius. The heart has gone out of the world, and the unheroic subject will take over from the citizen.

Julius Caesar has prepared the way for monarchy and peace; within that peace can be sown the seeds of a new faith which exalts peace. The old gods leave with the last warrior.[3] The old order and its characteristic man must pass before the new one can grow. Caesar is the peak and the end of that old order. Republican Rome had existed and flourished on two conditions—external warfare and domestic faction. Caesar, in principle, ended both of these conditions, which are undesirable in themselves; in so doing, he rendered it no longer necessary to have Romans.

The important question is, then, what were Caesar's talents and what was the policy that brought about such results? As a preliminary step toward answering this question, we must look to the character of the Roman polity as delineated in the plays, for the heroes are faced with Roman problems. They understand themselves to be acting as Roman citizens; what they must be and do is determined by the laws of Rome.

The first thing we learn from both *Coriolanus* and *Julius Caesar* is that Rome is not one city, but two—the city of the rich and the city of the poor. These two cities form an alliance with a shifting balance of power; and it is in relation to this balance that the statesmen play their roles, set their courses, and show what they can do. There is no higher principle or interest that unites them; each is necessary to the other, but they are hostile to each other; and each moderates the goals of the other by sheer force. The city of the rich contains all that is noble and interesting; these are the men who make up the Senate and lead the wars. They are the soul of Rome. Shakespeare is no democrat. It is not, as we shall see, that he lacks sympathy for the poor; it is rather that he is convinced that certain important virtues can be possessed by only a few and that those few require special training and long tradition. It is this concentration on virtue, and particularly certain political virtues, that leads him to emphasize the special rights of the patricians. If political rights were to be equalized, as happened under Augustus, the virtues of the few would have no field of action. Rome is great by its senatorial class, and that class is really unique— a relatively large group of men who are sufficiently obedient to the laws to avoid both anarchy and the rule of a single man; who sacrifice ordinary weakness and self-indulgence to a strict military discipline, the rewards of which are only honors; and who alone can be trusted to conclude on the issues of war and peace. And this is not for a day, but has endured for hundreds of years. Among them, it seems possible for single individuals to work wonders; Roman history is not the history of huge, impersonal movements, but that of great individuals. The poor, the body of the nation, are tied to their physical needs; their visions are limited by necessity. They possess none of the qualities of statesmanship and are easily led and misled. They change their convictions on the slightest occasions; they are governed by fear; and, when they take on the airs of courage and wisdom, they are revealed to be slavish as soon as they are put to the test. This does not mean that Shakespeare hates them; he knows them to be, like most humans, largely weak, but not vicious. But one must face the facts, and, according to Shakespeare, the man who has greater qualities should be preferred to those who have lesser ones.

Coriolanus failed because he could not handle the people; Caesar succeeded because he betrayed his own class and won the people by appealing to what is basest in them. This is the hidden theme of the Roman plays—the corruption of the people is the key to the mastery of Rome.

The people, under the Republic, really do control the city. They are free and participate in the election of magistrates, although they cannot themselves become magistrates. They possess a power of veto. The constitutional intention of their participation is obviously to prevent the rulers from following policies destructive of the people's interest. The people must be taken account of and not become slaves. This works perfectly as long as the senatorial class is unified and chooses its candidates for office on the basis of what they understand to be necessary for the city as a whole. In this case, the people's power only serves to ensure that a truly common good be found. But, as soon as a group of senators becomes corrupt and wishes to rule in ways and with powers contrary to the sense of the laws, they can appeal over the heads of their equals to the wishes of the people. The people cannot lead, but, as soon as a man who is powerful in the senatorial class can lead them, all is lost. Then the interests of the tyrant and the people rule in opposition to the class that represents virtue.

Both *Coriolanus* and *Julius Caesar* begin with the people, and in both cases they are understood to be the cause of the prevailing unrest. But the body of plebs is quite different in the two plays.[4] In *Coriolanus*, they are much more solid; the agitation arises because they are oppressed and hungry. Their demands are at least plausible, and they are largely motivated by fear that they will lose what little voice they have. They have just been conceded the establishment of tribunes to express their grievances to an indifferent Senate. They are not paragons, but seem to be ordinary rustic folk; they may not have been good warriors, but they had fought. There is every indication that their claims are legitimate and that Shakespeare has taken his cue from Plutarch, who insists that lack of consideration for the people was pushed to the point of a vice in Coriolanus.[5] In *Julius Caesar*, on the other hand, there is a lazy, brutal populace, a real urban proletariat. They are accustomed to dominating, and they are insolent; they have the habit of being flattered. How different were those plebs who feared that they were being made fun of by Coriolanus from these, who are the imperious arbiters of the civil war to whom the whole rhetoric of the conspiracy is directed. They are accustomed to bread and circuses; they change heroes according to how much is done for them. In *Coriolanus*, they are afraid of oppression; in *Julius Caesar*, they are indifferent to tyranny and are the causes of it. The people, when poor and held in check by the aristocrats, are perfectly decent and deserving of pity; when in control of the state, they are the enemies of republican institutions. The criticism of them implied in *Coriolanus* is that they are impetuous, in *Julius Caesar*, that they are heartless and fickle.[6] The tribunes in *Coriolanus* are vile self-seekers who mislead an innocent populace; their power depends on the people's hostility toward the senators and the traditional order. In *Julius Caesar*, the tribunes are courageous opponents of Caesar, protecting the people's interests against the people's wishes. The new Caesarean regime comes from members of the patriciate; in the name of the people, this new regime will suppress the power of the tribunes.[7] The tribunes are even put in the position of defending the traditional role of the senatorial class, so that the constitution can remain intact! This corruption in the character of the people and their relation to the senators is the measure of the distance between Coriolanus' Rome and Caesar's Rome.

Caesar holds the senators, his peers, in bondage owing to his control of the mob. Throughout the play, it is manifest that the cause of the senators is lost. They cannot unite among themselves, since any union would be quickly broken by those attracted to playing the demagogue and using the strength of the people to gain personal ascendancy. There is no hope of relying on the decency or patriotism of the plebs, for they are blind and corrupt beyond recall. They are incapable of distinguishing their flatterer from the good ruler. The only way to suppress Caesar would be to establish another tyranny. But why do that? The only dignity in the conspiracy comes from its insistence on freedom and legality. Another tyrant would probably be worse than Caesar.

This impasse is most beautifully brought out in the two funeral orations. Brutus speaks as a gentleman addressing gentlemen. His speech is in prose, and he appeals coldly, with no reference to reward, to the civic virtues of his audience. He treats them as old Romans; virtue is its own reward, and his listeners are presumed to possess an unselfish love of liberty. Antony's speech is in verse; he is a rhetorician. The more corrupt the audience, the more brilliant the rhetoric. A good citizen speaks the truth and respects his audience enough to believe they are competent to recognize the common good and virtuous enough to act in accordance with it. The flatterer assumes the baseness of his audience and appeals to its vices, cloaking his enticements in the beauty of his words. Brutus is austere; Antony, charming. And Antony's appeal is based solely on Caesar's benefactions to the people. Caesar could not be a criminal, for he loved the people; that is the sum of Antony's argument. When he gives promise of future reward of the grossest kind, his cause is won. All this he learned in the school of Caesar; Caesar knew how to use the people against the aristocrats, and that was the basis for ending all faction in the name of Caesarism. This play shows the last gasps of senatorial power or the coming-to-consciousness on the part of the old rulers that their day is done. Their edicts can no longer be enforced; they can either die or learn to live in comfortable obscurity.

I I

In order to come to grips with Caesar's character, it is well to cast a glance at his opposite number, Coriolanus. The light cast by Coriolanus' failure will illuminate Caesar's success. Coriolanus' greatness is of a sort that turned him from the best of citizens into a traitor condemned by his country; Caesar's greatness turns him from a traitor into the city's god.

Coriolanus' principle makes it impossible for him to deal with the people. It is a matter of simple pride. He is a gentleman, and gentlemen do not debase themselves in order to gain what they desire. Coriolanus, as a result of his public services, deserves to rule; hence, he should be given office without having to seek it or having to add to his sufficient title extraneous adornments that would please an unwise mob.[8] In all reason, if he is deserving, his refusal to flatter is justified. A decent city rewards decent men. If one must do what is base to gain honor, then the laws, with their noble precepts, would not be the guides to happiness or success; they would not be respectable. Put in another way, the laws or the way of life of a city are products of that group which is dominant in it. The good citizen is the man who best fits this regnant spirit. The virtues Coriolanus possesses fit the spirit of the senatorial class; if this class is the city, he is at home.[9] If the city is the people or some combination of plebs and patricians, he must moderate or alter his heroic character in order to fit and be honored. Coriolanus wants his kind of man to be dominant in the city; in this, at least, he does not differ from Socrates. What is the good of serving that which is not noble and will not permit him to remain noble? As a consequence of this opinion, he is required to deny the political existence of the great mass of the people.

In a way, Coriolanus' objections to the people are based merely on a prediction that, once admitted to a share in power, the ultimate results will be those we see in *Julius Caesar*. In reading his great diatribes against the people, one cannot help but be impressed with the reasonableness of the substance, if not of the style.[10] All of the accusations are accurate descriptions of the actions and thoughts of the people as Shakespeare describes them. But there is a difference in tone, if one can compare Shakespeare's presentation to that of Coriolanus. The latter is full of hatred and bitterness; there is almost what one would today call a reformer's spirit in Coriolanus' approach. Shakespeare indicates that he himself possesses a spirit of acceptance. That is the way things are, and there is no hope of reforming humanity. In this, Shakespeare, I believe, takes his cue from Plutarch. Plutarch blames Coriolanus, not for his opinion of the people, but for caring about them. He brings in as witness the gentle Aristides, who largely shared Coriolanus' estimation of the many, but who, for that very reason, expected nothing of them. He accepted with the same equanimity the archonship and ostracism. The difference between the two men is that Coriolanus is hungry for honor;[11] that is his deepest urge. He wishes to prove himself best. A man only knows himself best on the witness of others; he, as a Roman, must follow the *cursus honorum*, success in which is the sign of virtue.

However, this success now depends on the people, who vote according to their understanding and taste. To be attached to them is contemptible; they are not worthy judges. There is a myth that the man who obeys the laws and is courageous in war will be rewarded; actually, the man who is best adapted to the popular temper of his nation is the one who succeeds. Coriolanus' spirited nobility will not permit him to accept this fact. If easy deception is the road to honor, why should he engage in the difficult enterprises that made him famous? He wants competent judges of his merit; he wants Aufidius to be great so that he can defeat him;[12] he needs a world of heroes to fight so that he can be approved the hero among heroes. He does not want to win a cheating election that covers the true qualities of things; he wants others to admire him for what he really is. Coriolanus wants his virtue to be independent. But, in the decisive sense, he is dependent on the city, which is not virtuous, but is a composite of good and bad. All the honor that comes from it is tainted. This is Coriolanus' tragedy.

Coriolanus, extrapolating from the principles of a gentleman, in reality wants his virtue and honor to be those of a god. Gods are worshiped because they are powerful and good, not because they flatter the city. What they do for men they do freely and as a result of prayers; they are not needy. When Coriolanus is finally forced to the choice between a compromise and revolting against civil authority, he chooses the latter course. He believes that he can punish Rome for its ingratitude.[13] He takes on a horrible grandeur in his anger and is like a raging, merciless god— "He wants nothing of a god but eternity and a heaven to throne in." [14] But this moment is short-lived. Coriolanus without a political role is no Coriolanus, and, to live a political life, one must have a city to lead and to rule. Coriolanus no longer has a city. He can never return to Rome, because he hates it and because he would never again be trusted. And the city he thinks he is using for his revenge is in reality only using him; he has no place in it.[15]

All this is brought home to him when his mother comes to plead—this terrible woman who nurtured him to his pride. He loves her and pities her; she cannot live without the approval of Rome. Volumnia had never dreamed it possible that there could be a conflict between raising a proud, intransigent Roman and being a good citizen. She chooses the city when confronted with the choice between it and her son. Coriolanus' remaining contact with human sentiments is through his mother, and it is this weakness that destroys him. A god has no pity, because he is too far above the pains of humans to be threatened by them. His purpose cannot be altered by pleas; at least he cannot be forced to change. Coriolanus' attachment to his mother forces him to behave as a citizen. After all, Coriolanus was like other men, and he should not have aspired to rise so high.

Aristotle says that a man without a city is a god or a beast. Coriolanus, who made the attempt to live without a city, at first appears to be a god and proves to be a beast, slain in ambush like one.[16] He had no real source of power or humanity outside of Rome. The lesson to be drawn for our purposes is that a man cannot become a god, in Rome at least, on the patrician principles. The people's love is necessary; a god unworshiped is no god. The people's love is not won by mere heroic virtue. In other words, a man who wishes to become a god, who is conscious of the extent of his ambition, cannot behave as gods are popularly understood to behave. The base tribunes who fear that Coriolanus will become a god are able to prevent it; the noble tribunes and conspirators, in trying to forestall Caesar's becoming a god, are themselves destroyed.

I I I

Caesar had learned this well. He performed deeds as least as great as those of Coriolanus, but they were only steps on the road to the fulfillment of his dreams. Caesar's victories were used to subvert the constitution and get a hold on the people. He combined military force, to hold the Republic, with great generosity, to gain the love of the people. He knew that mere generosity or good deeds in the past would not suffice. The people had forgotten Pompey. But this union of force with courting of the people rendered the Senate completely impotent. No rival could muster enough of a following to challenge him. Caesar's control of the city of Rome, with all its prestige, was decisive in the civil war. This policy was doubly strong because, with the people as an ally, he had no rivals among them to fear. The people are easily satisfied;

only patricians, who live for the freedom and influence guaranteed to their position by the constitution, feel the consequences of having a single ruler.

All this is subtle policy, but it comes from the soul of a man who is no gentleman; it is a policy of ruse, treachery, violence, and treason. All canons of loyalty and decency go by the board; virtue is only a means to the end of glory and is hence only accessory. What is remarkable is that this man, who cares so little for the conventional virtues, does not degenerate into mere self-indulgence, that he possesses the charms of nobility.

Caesar was ready to undergo every kind of degradation; he knew that he was in need of other men, men not gained by virtue. Coriolanus could understand himself as a man devoted to the common good; Caesar's selfishness is explicit. This is, of course, an old story, and it is far easier to espouse such a Caesarean policy than to pursue it. It only goes to show that Caesar's greatness had as its condition a neglect of ordinary legality and decency. Although the people praise the practice of the virtues, in deed they consider the good man to be the one who benefits and attribute all the virtues to him. This Caesar knew, and his genius was guided by this awareness. The man who tried to be faithful to the traditions of Rome and the highest principles of morality was inevitably a traitor to Rome; the man who broke every sacred law and cared not a whit for the simplest principles of faith became a god. The paradox of Caesar's character—a character capable of the highest ambition and the lowest deeds—is formulated by Montesquieu in Machiavellian fashion: "This extraordinary man had . . . many great qualities without a single defect, although he had many vices. . . ." [17]

Caesar's roots in the acclaim of the worst sort of citizen is the first stage in Shakespeare's ambiguous presentation of him. Caesar is a man who has built his palace on the ruins of the Republic. Of course, there is every indication that it was already very corrupt. But the man who takes advantage of corruption is not particularly admirable, and one who destroys the manly equality of trusting friends and so gains his glory is a questionable figure.[18] Caesar is not like Romulus, who did disagreeable things in order to found the greatest of all republics. Whether Caesar intended to found anything is not clear, and what he did in fact found was distinctly inferior to what preceded.

On the other hand, to have overcome such rivals and to have found a formula that, in restoring peace between plebs and patricians, at the same time exalted himself, argues that he possessed no mean qualities. Even if they do not evoke respect, they do at least evoke wonder. It is often said that Caesar is a mere tyrant, and the play is understood to be a panegyric to the republican spirit and to tyrannicide.[19] This view, however, requires a selective reading of Caesar's interventions and forgets the obvious fact that the conspiracy ultimately fails. This failure is not just bad luck; it has to do with Caesar's strengths and Brutus' and Cassius' weaknesses. After all, the play ends with the punishment of the murderers and the triumph of the Caesarean party.

This in no sense implies that the interpretation which takes the conspiracy to be simply wicked is correct. But at least it begins from the broad lines presented by the play itself. The issue cannot be avoided by asserting that Shakespeare was only interested in the depiction of character and that the justice of the cause does not play a role in his thinking or in his play. Justice is part of a man's character, and Shakespeare knew it. One might suggest that the play takes for granted that there was something superior in the old Rome and that tyranny is a bad thing, but that Caesar's tyranny was something unique and that this was not properly grasped by the conspirators. Perhaps this individual, although inimical to constitutional and hence healthy regimes, is so superior that he deserves to rule no matter what. Perhaps our sympathies should be divided between respect for legitimacy and astonishment at Caesar's talents. Nothing says that there must be a harmony between civic morality and human greatness, and perhaps there was no alternative at that time and place. Then we would be forced to admire Caesar's political skill while honoring the dead—but always renewable—republican principles of the conspirators. It is this series of "perhaps's" that is the source of the obscurity of Shakespeare's intention.

It is possible to play Caesar as a petty, petulant, frightened despot, but it would be absurd to do so. There would then be no accounting for how Caesar had got where he is or for the general opinion that he was "the noblest man that ever lived in the tide of time." [20] I say that this opinion is general, although I quote from the mouth of Antony. Brutus has a similar esteem for him, and even those who hate Caesar never speak of him as anything but an exceptional individual. Cassius' tirade against him, with all its venom and rhetorical inflation, never describes Caesar as a minor man. Cassius simply insists that he is a man and that the differences in men cannot be so great as to allow one to rule all others, at least when there are Cassius's and Brutus's around.[21] The high point of his argument is that Brutus could conceive of himself as *equal* to Caesar. In the judgments of his contemporaries, Caesar is a very important personage, and not important in the sense in which a hereditary monarch is important. The latter must be reckoned with, not because of what he has himself accomplished, but merely because of the force of tradition, whereas Caesar has made his own situation and has the force to strengthen it.

Nor is he a tyrant in the sense of those who want the first position in order to indulge private lusts and for whom political power is merely a means of being free of the ordinary civil restrictions. Caesar's ambition is allied to a certain kind of public spirit; he wishes Rome to be happy and healthy under his leadership. Although his power is in the people, he respects the patricians and wants them to be his friends. He is still, in one way, the traditional Roman; he wants to win his glory from the free assent of the members of his class. He has made efforts to win them and has not merely purged all men of spirit, after the fashion of the tyrant. Brutus, a former opponent, stands high in his councils, and the dangerous Cassius is left undisturbed. The exquisite urbanity we know in the historical Caesar is to be found here, too.[22] We see examples of Caesar's astuteness and his high-minded lack of concern for his safety.[23] Much of the complaint against him stems from pique, vanity, and envy. Although some of his speeches smack to us of bombast, it is not so clear that this was Shakespeare's intention, for ours is not an age that takes well to speech of the heroic variety. There is a certain distance in manner and a pride in expression necessary to the leader, especially the leader in civil strife.

So much for the more extreme charges against Shakespeare's Caesar.[24] But there is also no question that there is a certain disproportion between Caesar's rhetoric about himself and what little we see of him in action. He says that he is not touched by fear; but he gives way, if not to his own fears, at least to those of his wife. And he delivers his marvelous speech about being unmovable just after we have seen him moved by flattery.[25] Finally, in desiring a crown and the title of king, he seems guilty of imprudence. The people, who are serving under a monarch, do not wish to be aware of a situation which they themselves have created. Names mean everything to the people, and substance, nothing. Caesar appears to affront this sentiment unnecessarily, since he already holds all the real power of a king. There is something petty in his desire, however logical a consequence it may be of his own ambitions. It is the cause of the conspirators' final resolution.[26]

It might be suggested that the real, live Caesar who confronts us is a man at the end of his career. He has accomplished all he has to do. There are few great actions left; he has only to reap vain honors. He has triumphed over all possible opponents, and with a certain sadness sees that his equals are no longer his equals. Pompey is dead, and there is no Aufidius, for all the Volscians have been conquered. In spite of his moderation and generosity, he cannot trust those around him. There is no way to distinguish true love from the blandishments of the frightened and interested; he does control by arms, not love. He lives only on words, his own and others. One can hardly imagine that such a man could settle down to the career of a peaceful public administrator. All that remains is the last forbidden fruit, the crown, the opposition to which was the vital center of the Republic's history. We see the glowing ashes of a Caesar who has been consumed in his passion for glory. He is now indecisive and prone to error. What is left is his own vision of what he wanted to be and how he should be understood by others.[27]

Caesar conceives of himself as a god. Unlike mortals, his will is not determined by reason; his will is sufficient reason.[28] This is the sign of omnipotence. In his last speech, when he is closest to the apprehension of mortality, he compares himself to the immortals. Among his last words before the attack are, "Wilt thou move Olympus." [29] Then he disappears forever. One might think that this was the clearest proof of Caesar's pride and the fitting punishment for it. But, in reality, the conspirators have made him into a god. They have saved him from the errors of humanity and its weaknesses. The position he had created was too great to be filled by a man, even Caesar; but Caesar's spirit, once released from his body, ranged over the wide world. The conspirators prevented Caesar from making the final error of allowing himself to be called king. Instead, they made it possible for kings to be honored to be called "Caesar."

Caesar's name became identical with monarchy of the grandest kind. His own person would not have sufficed to this role; but the edifice carefully constructed by him *plus* the memory of his martyrdom formed an almost eternal imperium. If the republican conspirators had not slain him, he might well have gained the odium of most Romans, as is indicated by the people's initial reaction to the tendering of the crown. The conspiracy saved Caesar from himself. From the moment the daggers are withdrawn from the corpse, Caesar's spirit comes alive to dominate the rest of the play's action.[30]

I V

Caesar required honor upon honor in order to live; universal empire was the fulfillment of his ambitions. Only the situation of a god could satisfy his thirst, and he did achieve this satisfaction—eternal fame and worship.[31] But, humanly, he wanted the free and honest admiration of the best men of his time, and this he did not get. As a man, he was a failure; his tragedy is consummated in seeing the Roman senators—and particularly the most virtuous of them all, Brutus—he had so sedulously courted attack him. To be Caesar is no solution to the problem of leading a noble political life that is not tragic, not rooted in fundamental contradictions. But no political man is his equal.

It is in the analysis of this alliance of senators that Shakespeare teaches the tragedy of Caesar and of Rome. It was formed to put an end to Caesar's endless ambition and restore a Rome in which men had ruled and been ruled by one another in turn, a Rome in which the pride of equality among equals and submission to the laws was the theme and where individual deeds had unlimited possibilities and an exalted significance. The alliance failed, and this failure is due, on the one hand, to the skill of Caesar's work and, on the other hand, to the inadequacies of the conspirators. We are shown the hearts and the minds of the conspirators, and we become aware of the awesome talents that would have been required to make the conspiracy succeed and what the imperfections were that doomed it. Shakespeare telescopes history so as to draw out its true significance, and he leaves nothing to accident. The actors and their faults are everything; material circumstances and chance are reduced to an almost meaningless minimum.

The conspiracy has two leaders, and they are responsible for the execution of the plot. Shakespeare has centered the whole action around them and has done so to an even greater degree than did his source, Plutarch. They act in the name of all Rome, in particular in the name of the senatorial class. Casca is given as the model of the decent, blunt, independent men who are typical of that class. Those who follow are the Casca's, but what they follow is the product of Brutus and Cassius. These two are special types who differ extremely and whose capacities complement each other but also bring them into crucial conflict. Brutus and Cassius are necessarily mated, for, without either one, it is inconceivable that the conspiracy should have begun at all. They are, however, too diverse to work together in complete harmony; their principles produce different policies. They would have to have been in complete concord to succeed; but that is very like an impossibility, because nature has made them so opposite. The plot should have been led by one man who had the qualities of both Brutus and Cassius. But how could nature have made such a monster? The sign of this natural impossibility is that one is a self-announced Stoic and the other a self-proclaimed Epicurean—the two opposite poles in philosophical sectarianism. Could a man be both Stoic and Epicurean?

The motivations of both Brutus and Cassius are truly republican, with the difference that, according to the formula of the time, the one hated tyranny, and the other, tyrants.[32]

Brutus believed in legitimacy, in the traditional Roman order. Cassius could not endure having to accept a master. Both positions reflect elements in the republican character; the one represents the principles, the other, the passions which must be combined for a republican regime to endure. Brutus' reasons for participation seem more public-spirited and better grounded in virtue. Cassius is apparently pursuing a private grudge, but his response to his private passion is a strong and free one. Both Brutus and Cassius are noble Romans, the sort of men who made republican Rome the glory of political history.

Cassius is the animator of the plot. He has the idea, and he organizes everything. Conspiracies are low things; they require secrecy and stealth. As such, they are not the best ground for gentlemen, who are not in the habit of hiding anything or of feeling the shame that seeks the cover of darkness. This does not bother Cassius.[33] Caesar is a tyrant; there are no lawful means to do justice to a tyrant who has usurped all lawfulness. Therefore, he must be done away with. His view of the end dictates the means, and he moves clear-headedly toward the goal without conscience. Cassius needs no painful dialectic with himself to prove that it is right for gentlemen to commit murder. He is much more sanguinary than his colleague, and his colleague has only become his colleague because he has been subtly corrupted by Cassius. It is also not the office of a gentleman to deceive a man who is supposed to be his friend. But Cassius wants Brutus in on the assassination, so he feels no compunction about presenting him with images which will appeal to his ambition, an ambition so pure that its highest object is to gain the reputation for virtue.[34] Why does the able and courageous Cassius want to associate himself with the pure Brutus? The answer is that Cassius needs Brutus, for Brutus has the reputation for virtue which will draw other worthy men into the conspiracy, and, after the assassination, only he could make the deed appear to the people to be good and just.[35] Virtue is necessary to political success; it is a weapon. The reputation for honor and justice is not gained in a day; Cassius may be a clever statesman, but his very cleverness has made it impossible for him to acquire the reputation for virtue. This conspiracy needs a reputation which can equal Caesar's, as well as a prudence to match his. Cassius needs Brutus for the sake of public opinion.

Brutus is a man who loves virtue, who only asks himself what the right thing to be done is. He does not, like Cassius, calculate what advantage will accrue to him if he behaves rightly. He is not a regular fellow; he seems cold; but he is the sort of man to whom others turn in cases where trust is important. He demands much of others, but also of himself. He applies the strictest rules of justice and does not mitigate them out of friendship or pity. Brutus is truly a Stoic. For that reason, since reputation is so important in political things, less just men are tempted to try to use him as a front to mask their schemes or to give an air of respectability to their selfish motives. Caesar prized his friendship, and Cassius tries to seduce him.

In addition to being a virtuous man, Brutus is also eminently a political animal. He is no less political than Cassius, who sees all happiness and joy in exercising the rights of a Roman citizen. Brutus understands virtuous conduct to be that of a wise and sober counselor and judge. Just as Cassius, from the point of view of his philosophy, could have chosen a life of voluptuary satisfaction and turned his back on political honors, so Brutus, too, from the point of view of his philosophy, could have chosen the life of the solitary sage who studies nature indifferent to the passing currents of political life. But he did not become a sage because virtue, to him, is incorporated in the life of the good citizen. He despises honor; he is apparently insensitive to what moves Caesar and Cassius. However, he can hardly be imagined outside the role of statesman and general; without the occasion for the exercise of those activities, Brutus could not be virtuous and hence happy. It is a mistake to say that Brutus is a theoretical man not made for political practice. Undoubtedly, his notion of the virtues makes it difficult for him to act prudently in extreme situations, but that does not mean that this notion is not fundamentally political or that Brutus can live in any other world than that of the city and its dispensing of justice. He apparently has shown himself competent in a life devoted entirely to politics. The fact that he reads books does not prove that there is anything philosophic in him; it might only indicate that he is somewhat bookish. He, as much as the other characters in the play, has the passion for politics coursing through his veins.

Brutus brings respectability, calm, and resolve to the conspiracy. Nobody can question this; since he is not afraid of consequences, once he has made up his mind, he is unshakable. Cassius has doubts and terrors and sometimes is disposed to act rashly.[36] With Brutus, the only difficulty is in deciding to do the deed. But this is not easy. His Stoic calm disposes him to accept the evils of the time. He is, above all men, indebted to Caesar. Finally, murder is contrary to his principles. In his reflections on the problem, we see his characteristic mode of reasoning and penetrate the difficulties of the moral stance which ultimately makes him so disastrous a partner in crime. He reasons in terms of how the killing of Caesar can be justified to the public, how it will receive the "color" of morality.[37] Brutus is determined on action because the deed is one that can be justified in terms of the public understanding of virtue. For Cassius, it is sufficient to hate serving another human being; the Stoic Brutus could never accept the judgment of the selfish passions; rather, one should change those passions. Only reasons will do. But what are sufficient reasons? It seems that they are those which can satisfy the public at large. Brutus will not act out of self-love; he prides himself on acting contrary to the movements of his heart. But he will act according to the popular view of what is decent, not because he hopes to be popular. but because he has no other source of knowledge about what is decent.

Brutus' situation can be characterized in this way: he believes that to be virtuous is to be happy. If one obeys the laws of virtue without fail, it makes no difference whether one has any of the external goods. But what is virtue? In answer to this question, he can only respond: what is held to be virtuous. He is so completely a political man that he cannot conceive of a virtuous life which is not the life of a Roman senator. But this means that virtue is not really a completely individual possession; one must belong to a city. Brutus' virtue is not an unknown or private virtue, like that of the most authentic Stoics, who took Diogenes as one of their supreme models. Brutus, as we learn, really admits that happiness requires conditions in addition to virtue. He believes that one must have a city in which to exercise virtue, or, otherwise put, one must have some political honor. A city draws its moral principles from its laws, and the laws and their spirit are what Brutus truly listens to. But what never seems to occur to him is that, on occasion, those laws need forbidden, unlawful actions for their maintenance. Caesar and Cassius are only too aware of this fact; injustice may be the condition of justice or happiness. It is only too clear why Brutus does not consider this possibility: if there are no permanent principles of justice, if virtue requires supplements which are not virtuous, if to be a good man and a happy one are at least potentially different things, then how would one choose between them? Brutus' calm superiority to base considerations and his freedom from anxiety about the conditions of happiness rest on the conviction that morality is absolute.

The murder of Caesar is, of course, a great break with the absoluteness of Brutus' principles, and it is only after a struggle with himself that he brings himself to undertake it. It is doubtful whether he ever really permits himself full consciousness of what he has done. In reality, he tries to convert the deed into something other than what it is. He understands it to be a sacrifice to the gods, the sources of morality.[38] Even if he does see that this is an extraordinary, extramoral deed, he is unwilling to draw the obvious consequence. This consequence is that, once one has performed such a deed, one must do all that is necessary to make it effective; the old rules do not apply, since one is already outside the rules. Instead, Brutus reverts immediately to his stringent principles and lets the consequences be damned, even though Caesar has been killed for the consequences which might follow from his power. Brutus assumes that Romans will behave morally, although Caesar has won his position by corrupting them. It is Brutus' unwillingness to embark on a stormy political sea without a moral compass that leads him to make several errors. These errors are all committed over Cassius' opposition. Shakespeare has contrasted the two men with almost geometric precision in each case, and the failure of the plot can be directly traced to the victory of Brutus' principles over Cassius' prudence.

Brutus refuses to admit Cicero into the plot; he refuses to

kill Antony; he insists that Antony be permitted to speak at
Caesar's funeral; he opts to do battle immediately, rather
than delay.[39] Cassius wanted to do otherwise in each question. In two of the cases, Cassius was the initiator of the contrary policy and was overriden by Brutus. In two instances,
public opinion is alleged as the motive for disagreeing with
Cassius; in the third, fortune and its effects on human policy
is the reason;[40] and, in the fourth, Brutus alleges that Cicero's vanity makes it impossible for him to be a follower,
which means, since Brutus is the acknowledged leader, that
he wants no challenge to his leadership. Although a plausible
and moral ground can be made for each of Brutus' decisions, each can be referred to the more ambiguous sides of
his character—the moral self-confidence and the urge for
public respectability. He pays scant attention to Cassius, of
whose qualities he is less aware than Cassius is of his. Cassius always gives in, almost without discussion. It might be
a cause of wonder why he does so, since he is so conscious of
his own intellectual clarity. The answer is Brutus' moral superiority. Cassius cannot hope to prevail in an open conflict,
for the others would follow Brutus without question. They
trust him. More important, Cassius' lack of principle gives
him a certain lack of will. The conviction of one's own virtue
is a source of strength. Brutus believes that he is self-
sufficient, whereas Cassius is only too aware of his own dependence. Morality is a real force, and Cassius is intimidated
by it.

Let us now look at the errors themselves more closely. No
proof is required to assert that it was an act of gross conspira-
torial stupidity to leave Mark Antony alive. The denouement
is enough for that. Mark Antony was the heir to Caesar's
teaching and could certainly not be trusted. Similarly, the
funeral oration was the means to arouse the people, the
source of Caesar's power. In one way, Brutus' gentleness can
be regarded as a virtue; he was too good for this world. He
wanted to do away with the evil without making the cure
worse than the disease. Cassius' policy would have led to
bloody purges. Looked at in another way, Brutus is culpably
weak, given the importance of the issue at stake; gentleness
can be seen as a kind of self-indulgence. At all events, by
saving Antony, Brutus saved Caesar. Further, Brutus' precip-

itousness to begin the battle is clearly mistaken. Appian's assertion that the argument presented by Cassius is correct is not even necessary; Octavius himself says that what Brutus does is precisely the thing their party wants.[41]

Finally, although it is less easy to detect the error involved in the rejection of Cicero, I believe that Shakespeare's presentation of the great orator is such as to indicate that his taking part would have been a decisive asset. We learn from hearsay that Cicero is a subtle man who knows how to mask his sentiments and that he, like Brutus, would add respectability to the conspiracy, although he is regarded for his judgment, rather than for his nobility. The one glimpse we get of him is most revealing. Casca meets him in the midst of the great storm which seems to give cosmic support to the unrest within Rome. Casca is struck with awe; he is a moral man and a superstitious one. The gods, the guardians of morality, are sending signs. Cicero is calm and unmoved and implies that he does not believe that these storms have anything to do with human affairs. He remains reasonable, whereas the religious Casca gives himself over to tormented speculations. Casca then meets Cassius, who is also a non-believer, but whom the storm has stimulated to wild impiety and defiance of the heavens. He uses the events to intensify the hostility to Caesar. Cicero is a golden mean in the scene between the terrified believer and the fanatic unbeliever. He is not a man to see ghosts, nor is he one who has renounced morality. Perhaps he could have mediated between Brutus' moral passion and Cassius' calculation.

Given that Cicero might have possessed talents deserving of a place in the plot, what would have been the result of his participation? Whether he would have been the leader or not, it is hardly to be believed that the man universally acknowledged the greatest orator in Roman history would not have presented the reasons for the assassination at Caesar's funeral. Brutus' speech was a failure and wrongly conceived, and we know, and Shakespeare could have known, that the real Cicero disapproved of Brutus' rhetoric. Would Cicero have so widely missed the mark? I doubt it.[42]

A single thread can be seen running through all Brutus' errors. It comes best into view in his objections to doing away with Antony. Antony is only Caesar's limb; all one needs to do is kill Caesar's spirit, and the body will die. Brutus wishes that he could kill Caesar's spirit without touching his body. But we have learned that Caesar's spirit is very much in the body and inseparable from it. Indeed, it can be said that his spirit lives in that part of the city which is most body. Caesar more than anyone knew that the soul must have material manifestations in order to have political significance; a great spirit must produce courageous armies and quantities of money. In a way, Brutus knows this, but his doctrine makes him forget it. He does not believe in the importance of external goods; strength of soul is all that counts. This is a salutary and inspiring doctrine, but it is not true. Caesar's spirit lives on in his arms. Brutus systematically underrates the importance of what is lowest—the body. Cassius vainly tells him that their opponents will starve if given time. But for Brutus "there is a tide in the affairs of men which taken at the flood leads on to success . . ."; he believes that his spirit and resolve will carry all before them.

His rejection of Cicero and his granting permission to Antony to speak reveal the same bias in an even deeper sense. Rhetoric is not important; honest men speak the truth to one another without ornament. A depreciation of rhetoric is a depreciation of the importance of the passions and of the distortions they effect on reason. He who knows rhetoric knows the people, and the people are the body of the state. Cassius, the materialist, the Epicurean, tries vainly to point this out to Brutus. It is true that Cassius thinks that everything is body, and he therefore misses something Brutus sees. But he is closer to an understanding of the extremities of politics than is the stoic Brutus, with his unshakable conviction that the soul's virtues are sufficient in themselves, not only for the wise man but for cities as well.

Up to this point, Brutus' faults, if they can be called such, are so bound up with all his good qualities that they possess a certain charm and might incline one to believe that there is only a choice between sweet but somewhat blind virtue and malignant prudence. In this light, Brutus would be vindicated. However, these failings take on a somewhat more somber cast in the quarrel with Cassius.[43]

This dispute is the most terrible and most touching moment in the drama. Here these last two hopes of Roman freedom meet, and it becomes clear that they cannot understand each other, although they love each other and their cause. The unity of the alliance is strained, and we see the seams of what is supposed to be a perfect unity. It is finally patched together, but the articulation of the disharmony is unforgettable. The two men confront each other with reproaches— reproaches which are, on each side, in character. Cassius is guilty of corruption or at least of winking at it. Brutus is guilty, if that is the word for it, of too much probity and a justice that is too severe for the circumstances. What is more, he overbears with all his morality. He, unlike Cassius, is so confident of his righteousness that he has no afterthoughts. Brutus dominates, and dominates cruelly, in the ensuing discussion. He feels himself "arm'd so strong in honesty" that he can despise Cassius' taunts and accusations. Poor Cassius obviously cares deeply for his friend and wants him to reciprocate; above all, he wants to avoid a final break. Brutus does not care; just as long as he is right. Cassius' bitter sense of impotence is moving, as he casts himself again and again against this rock of a man.

To this point in the play, Brutus has, in spite of subterranean flaws, been the distinctly superior person, and Cassius has appeared as a rather low figure, even comparable in some respects to Iago. But the roles suddenly begin to be reversed. Brutus, after castigating Cassius' "itching palm," in a turnabout accuses him of not having provided money when asked. Brutus himself is too good to squeeze the poor peasants. But he still needs the money, and he is perfectly willing to use Cassius' vice for his needs. He is unwilling to face the implications of his own situation and is forced into a rather ugly form of hypocrisy. Brutus remains pure by allowing others to perform the immoral acts which are the conditions of his purity. Then he can attack Cassius for being immoral. Wars need money, and, if a man starts a war, he is responsible for the acts which provide the money to pursue it, whether or not he performs them himself. Money is the sign of the material, or of what satisfies the needs of the body. Again Brutus refuses to recognize the existence of the body; in this instance, however, we are made privy to the casuistry, the falseness, into which such a man is forced. He does not really live on his virtue alone; he just acts as though he does.

Two further incidents heighten the somewhat sinister light which has been cast on Brutus. At the end of the quarrel, a poet bursts in on the pair. He wishes to use his poetry to produce harmony. Cassius is amused, but Brutus is vexed. "What have the warres to do with these jigging fools." Real life is too serious for poetry; Brutus shares the taste of the people who slew Cinna the Poet for his bad verses. This poet is a Cynic, and Cynics were the most unpolitical of men; they would not let their happiness be disturbed by the fall of nations. Poetry is a dimension of human life at a certain remove from the political. It is closer to those self-sufficient joys which look down on all that is merely political. Brutus is hostile to poetry in his monolithic moral intensity, and this is allied to his indifference to rhetoric. If Cassius hears no music, Brutus hears no poetry.[44]

This little scene is only a prelude to the most significant revelation about Brutus. When Brutus and Cassius have been reconciled, Brutus admits that he is "sick of many griefs," to which Cassius responds. "Of your philosophy you make no use/if you give place to accidental evils." Cassius does not say this in the spirit of theoretical disputation. He wants Brutus to be a Stoic; he needs a stoic Brutus; he wishes that his Stoicism were real. There is, buried in this comment, a grain of respect for Brutus' principles; he is not just benighted in the eyes of the Epicurean. Cassius does not try to convert his friend to his own creed, but urges that he live up to his beliefs. One suspects that Cassius feels his own beliefs to be low and that he admires the strength of the Stoic, that he is an Epicurean because he feels that he is not good enough to be a Stoic.

At all events, in his defense, Brutus reveals that Portia is dead. This is indeed a terrible loss, and we have seen what a wonderful couple they were. No one can deny that Brutus bears it bravely. But, according to strict Stoic doctrine, the loss of a wife is only an accidental evil, and it is a sign of corruption to care too intensely. If a man can be made unhappy by the death of loved ones, it means he is dependent on things beyond his control; virtue is not self-sufficient. We know that Brutus has unusual self-control. But self-control is an ambiguous faculty; it can be used to suppress the good with the bad. His doctrine is that the externals do not count. Actually they do count—we have seen it in the scene with Portia and elsewhere—and Brutus merely suppresses his sentiments, at great cost. Nothing in the thought which is the result of all his study and reflection and for which he is reputed can account for the sentiments he now experiences.

Immediately afterward, Titinius and Messala enter the tent, and Messala asks whether Brutus has heard of Portia. Brutus says no, plays the innocent, and lets Messala tell him the terrible news again. He responds with an edifying moralism and turns to other business. Cassius supports him in this deception and promotes the impression Brutus' apparent strength creates, almost as though he were putting him on display like a circus performer. Perhaps Brutus can be justified by saying that he must do this for the sake of maintaining his leadership, which requires a certain amount of ruse and myth. But there is, nonetheless, something ugly about using Portia's death in this way, as a means of giving the impression that he possesses a mastery that he does not actually have. This sums up Brutus' Stoicism; it is largely a public display which he uses to deceive others and himself. It is the counterpart of the Brutus who doubts in private but who, as soon as he steps on the public scene as the leader of the conspiracy, is assurance itself. The same man who in soliloquy could find no present reason to kill Caesar is able to speak with certitude and horror of "the time's abuse" when he addresses his fellows.[45]

Shakespeare underlines all this in the discussion between Brutus and Cassius about defeat and suicide. Brutus insists that defeat will not cause him to alter his philosophy. Just as he blamed Cato for doing away with himself rather than surrender to Caesar, he cannot countenance giving way before fortune's strokes. He will have the courage to continue living as he always has. But, as soon as Cassius calls up to him the image of being led in triumph to Rome, he declares that he would rather take his life. When it comes down to it, he is like any other noble Roman senator; honor and dishonor in the eyes of the city are what constitute the notions of good and bad. In this case, Brutus knows that his virtue will not win him honor. This is an extreme case, but principles are only seen in their true lights in the extreme.[46]

Brutus' Stoicism lends him a moral superiority in the eyes of the public and in his own eyes. It produces a self-confidence in action and a general probity of conduct. But the standard it sets is too high for human attainment; its adherents would perhaps be weaker if they took the passions more seriously, but they might also be more humane. True success will only be vouchsafed them when they have a true view of things.[47] The public example of virtue is necessary for civil society, and virtuous men deserve our praise, even if they fail. But the belief in a virtue that undermines the cause of justice and has no effects other than to add luster to one's reputation and to allow one to self-righteously avoid responsibility deserves less than our unqualified admiration. Brutus, as a result of his philosophy, thinks too well of himself. This philosophy vouchsafes him a stature beyond that of his colleagues, and his sweet nature moves those who see him in his privacy. But the two parts of his own nature do not cohere; he never really knows himself, and much of what is best in him goes counter to his beliefs. A true morality would have to take account of what causes him to love Portia, Lucius, and Rome.

Cassius, too, has given evidences of a loss of faith in his philosophy. But he avows it explicitly; the Cassius of acts IV and V is a very different man from the one we saw previously. He has become superstitious. He now believes that there are spirits and a providence in the world.[48] The man whose doctrine insisted that all action is selfish turns out to be the truest and most sentimental of friends. He even dies for friendship. In the most bitter of turnabouts, he dies for the memory of a friend who is not in fact dead and thereby destroys any possibility of reviving the alliance. His error is the result of his bad eyesight. Caesar had bad hearing but good eyes; Cassius, bad eyesight and good hearing. Caesar trusted more to what he saw than what he heard; Cassius trusted the report he heard about what another saw. The Epicurean, who depreciates hearsay and the senses, ruins everything because of his faith in the senses of others.[49] This is no true Epicurean; it is rather a man who has schooled himself in a teaching which ran counter to a fund of common goodness and ordinary political weakness within him. In Cassius, we see the case of a man who thinks worse of himself than he ought to and does so because he has accepted a philosophy which depreciates, discourages, and explains away what is good in him. In the final crisis, this arbitrary shell breaks, and the true man emerges. But it is too late.

In these last scenes of the play, what was a rigid opposition between Brutus and Cassius dissolves under the pressure of Caesar's unrelenting spirit, and they come closer to each other in their simple humanity. What has appeared bad now looks better, and what appeared good now looks somewhat worse. They are both good but erring men. Shakespeare does all of this very delicately so as not to disturb the superficial and roughly true structure of his message. What Brutus stands for is still better and more praiseworthy than what Cassius stands for. Shakespeare nevertheless severely shows the intelligent spectator why the plot must fail and demonstrates the inadequacies of ordinary men to overcome the force of a man like Caesar.

There is no other Shakespearean play in which the protagonists are explicitly followers of philosophic doctrines. With Brutus and Cassius, Shakespeare shows the impossibility of the direct application of philosophy to political affairs. Men are impressed with the doctrines of wise teachers who give them clarity about their world and help them chart a course that they themselves could not have drawn. But, in political practice, this results in abstractions, in neglect of the elusive unity of body and soul; reality is transformed to fit one's conceptions of it.

Neither Stoic nor Epicurean can explain the motivations of the characteristically political man who pursues glory through the city. The political man lives for neither wisdom nor pleasure, but for something in between; the city he serves is a mixture of high and low to which he must adjust. Caesar seems to have been the most complete political man who ever lived. He combined the high-mindedness of the Stoic with the Epicurean's awareness of the low material substrate of political things. Brutus and Cassius could not comprehend such a combination; faced with it, they simply lost their convictions. They could for a moment make headway against Caesar because of their alliance, but they ultimately contradicted each other. They were much simpler men than Caesar and would have been good citizens in a Rome where Caesars did not exist—a Rome where the laws, and not philosophies, gave them their guidance. A true philosophy would have to be supple enough to grasp the mind of Caesar—a difficult task, since he seems to defy the principle of contradiction. And such a philosophy would be of no use to men of practice, for it would provide them with no rules. Shakespeare gives a final word concerning his view of Stoicism and Epicureanism, or what we would call idealism and realism, in reference to politics. Political society does not exist for selfish ends, nor does it exist for virtuous ones. Neither doctrine will help. Both are in a way true; each is in its own way fatal.

Brutus and Cassius performed a most important function. Their failure, as Brutus saw, won them more glory than Octavius and Antony attained by their success, for they are the eternal symbols of freedom against tyranny. They showed that men need not give way before the spirit of the times; they served as models for later successors who would re-establish the spirit of free government. Their seemingly futile gesture helped, not Rome, but humanity. Men in foreign lands and with foreign tongues have looked to Rome and to the defenders of its liberties against Caesarism for inspiration in the establishment of regimes which respect human nature and encourage a proud independence.[50] Shakespeare, the teacher of the Anglo-Saxon world, was such a man. He saw that the times were against Brutus and Cassius; but their cause was right. New times and new energies might resurrect what is best in ancient Rome. Brutus and Cassius were good men and types which any polity should boast of producing. The next time, however, they would need a mind comparable to that of Julius Caesar to teach them and lead them.

NOTES

[1] Plutarch, *Julius Caesar*, trans. North (London: Nonesuch, 1930), III. 453. In the Greek, *daimon* ("divinity," or "genius") is the word trans-

lated by ". . . prosperitie and . . . fortune." This is what is meant by Caesar's "spirit."

2 Johann Peter Eckermann, *Conversations with Goethe*, January 31, 1827.

3 *Antony and Cleopatra* IV. iii. 16-26; vi. 7-9; I. ii. 29-33. All references to the text of *Julius Caesar*, *Coriolanus*, and *Antony and Cleopatra* are to the Furness variorum editions (Philadelphia: Lippincott, 1913, 1928, 1907).

4 The Roman plays are the only ones in which the people as a whole is an actor. Shakespeare grasped the republican genius well; he seems to see the character of the mass of people as particularly important in such a regime. The unresolved problem of the proper hierarchical ordering of the two parts of the city seems to be both its strength and its weakness, a perpetual tension that could be resolved only in the destruction of the Republic. This presentation is not unlike that of Machiavelli, *Discourses* I. iii-vi. Cp. *Coriolanus* I. i. 3-172 with *Julius Caesar* I. i., and *Coriolanus* II. iii. 1-187 with *Julius Caesar* III. ii-iii. The difference between the two periods is perhaps best underlined by the generous opinions of some of the plebs about their oppressor, Coriolanus.

5 Plutarch, *Comparison of Alcibiades with Coriolanus, op. cit.*, I, 427.

6 In *Julius Caesar*, cp. the tribunes' forthright, "you blocks, you stones . . ." (I. i. 44), with Antony's flattery, "You are not stones . . ." (III. ii. 152). Cp. I. ii. 294-295 with ". . . men forget more easily the death of their father than the loss of their patrimony" (Machiavelli *Prince* xvii).

7 I. ii. 305-307.

8 I. i. 179-200; II. ii. 160-170; iii. 41-143.

9 III. i. 238-248.

10 III. i. 84-201.

11 Plutarch, *Comparison* . . . , *op. cit.*, pp. 430-431; cp. II. ii. 9-24.

12 I. i. 255-258.

13 Coriolanus banishes Rome (III. iii. 151-166). Although Coriolanus previously seemed to speak for legality and the proper respect for tradition, he was always really a revolutionary. Rome had always had a plebeian class, and this class had long had certain privileges, e.g., the very right of electing the consuls to which Coriolanus objects so much. His passion to have a Rome without the abuses he sees leads him to contemplate the most extreme measures (II. iii. 117-129).

14 V. iv. 22-24. Coriolanus behaves, and is treated, as a god; IV. vi.-V. iii. 198. He is mentioned in relation to gods at II. i. 296-304; III. i. 103-104, 313-315; IV. v. 199-204; vi. 115-120, 125-127.

15 IV. vii. 58-59.

16 V. vi. 134-158. Menenius says that he has become a dragon from a man (V. iv. 11-14). He compares the change to that from a grub to a butterfly, which calls to mind two previous references to butterflies (I. iii. 61-69; IV. vi. 119); Coriolanus and his son pursued butterflies and tortured them. Ultimately, the proud pursuer turns into the bestial pursued, a mere "gilded butterfly."

17 *Grandeur des Romains*, xi.

18 It should not be forgotten that the triumph celebrated in the beginning

of the play was one gained over noble Roman citizens. To declare a
triumph for such a conquest was without example (I. i. 37-64).

19 It cannot be argued that Caesar was not a tyrant. This does not mean
that he was necessarily a bad man; tyranny is the exercise of illegiti-
mate powers illegitimately acquired. Such a man must necessarily be
hated by all good citizens who love the laws. Caesar surely exercised
such powers (III. i. 39-40), and his desire for a crown and a son
to wear it are the attempts to establish a new legitimacy. The attack
on Caesar is not comparable to the attack on a king; he is not surrounded by the holy aura of legitimacy. The only question is the
efficacy of the action.

20 III. i. 286-287.

21 I. ii. 158-171; II. i. 22-23; III. ii. 20-25; IV. iii. 19-20, 115-117.

22 II. ii. 124-140.

23 I. ii. 211-234, 30-31; III. i. 13.

24 The two instances of superstition of which so much is made to Caesar's
disadvantage by many critics are not such as to prove that this was
a real weakness. The belief that being touched by one of those who
run in the Lupercalia festival would make Calphurnia fertile is no
more than a traditional opinion, of which Caesar makes mention on
the appropriate occasion (I. ii. 4-14). The discussion with Calphurnia
about the ill omens of the time does not indicate that he really believes these portents to have meaning. He gives an example of his
mode of interpreting portents when he hears that an offering has no
heart. It merely supports his intended course of action. Caesar always knew how to make piety fit his purposes (II. ii. 3-101). He
does give in to his wife, but this has other grounds. And he accepts
an interpretation of his wife's dream which is akin to his own interpretation of the heartless offering. Even admitting that Caesar
does have a grain of superstition, perhaps this is a part of the great
political man's nature. The political life depends so much on chance,
on circumstances that reason can never control or predict, that the
statesman may well have to believe in some guiding spirits to
hearten him. A belief in one's fortune seems to go along perfectly
well with the political character and in no wise to contradict rational
policy.

Caesar's physical weakness, to which Cassius alludes and of which
we have one example given us and of another a reliable report, only
go to render Caesar's spiritual dominance more impressive and more
enigmatic (I. ii. 105-146, 268-275, 232-233). Cassius, the Epicurean,
errs in believing that the body is all there is to the man.

25 II. ii. 38-65, 94-118; III. i. 44-83.

26 "But the chief cause that made him mortally hated, was the covetous
desire he had to be called king: which first gave the people just
cause, and next his secret enemies, honest colour to beare him ill
will." Plutarch, *Julius Caesar, op. cit.*, pp. 445-446.

27 "Some of Caesar's friends entertained a suspicion that he neither
desired nor cared to live any longer, on account of his declining
health . . ." (Suetonius *Julius Caesar* 86).

M. W. MacCallum, in his exceptionally sensitive understanding of the play, describes the Caesar we see as follows: "In this assumption of the Divine, involving as it does a touch of unreality and falsehood, he has lost his old surety of vision and efficiency in act. He tries to rise above himself, and pays the penalty by falling below himself, and rushing on the ruin which a little vulgar shrewdness would have avoided. But his mistake is a clue to his very greatness, and his greatness encompasses him to the last . . ." (*Shakespeare's Roman Plays* [London: Macmillan, 1919], p. 231).

28 II. ii. 82-83.

29 III. i. 85.

30 Cassius thinks that Caesar is already a god (I. ii. 130-131) and that in slaying Caesar he will slay the god. But mortals are never gods, and gods cannot be slain. If there is any single impression which remains after reading or seeing this play, it is that Caesar's spirit is the true protagonist. Brutus and Cassius, able men with serious plans, are drowned in a force whose power they could not imagine. Antony releases the spirit (III. i. 300-303); it appears twice to Brutus, and the two principals in the conspiracy die with Caesar's name on their lips. The fullest tragic consciousness Brutus attains is with his, "O, Julius Caesar, thou art mighty yet" (V. iii. 106).

Dio Cassius tells that Brutus died reciting these lines, said to have been spoken by Heracles:

Wretched Virtue, you exist only in speech, while
I practiced you in deed; but you were only a slave to fortune.
Roman History XLVII 2.

This does not express any consciousness that Brutus himself has, but a Brutus could conceivably have made such a statement at the tragic end of a life devoted to his principles.

31 "He died in the fifty-sixth year of his age, and was ranked amongst the gods, not only by a formal decree, but in the belief of the vulgar" (Suetonius *Julius Caesar* 88).

32 Plutarch, *Marcus Brutus*, *op. cit.*, IV, 441-442.

33 I. iii. 138-142; cf. Brutus' reaction to stealth, II. i. 89-97.

34 I. ii. 57-193, 331-346.

35 I. iii. 171-182.

36 III. i. 19-32.

37 II. i. 13-37.

38 II. i. 193.

39 II. i. 159-173, 174-212; III. i. 252-281; IV. iii. 223-256.

40 Plutarch says that Brutus wanted the battle because he was anxious to have done, one way or the other (*Brutus*, *op. cit.*, p. 466). Shakespeare seems to indicate only optimism, which follows the burden of his characterization of Brutus. In either case, Brutus' apparent lack of attachment to and interest in the things of this world, as they present themselves naturally to political men, makes him imprudent.

41 *Civil Wars* IV. 108, 112, 122-123; *Julius Caesar* V. i. 3-8.

42 Cicero is mentioned four times (I. ii. 299-300; I. iii. 3-43; II. i. 159-173; IV. iii. 201-205). In the last reference, we learn that Cicero was one of those put to death by the Triumvirs; Antony will not make the same mistake Brutus does. It is also to be noted that Cicero seems

to be particularly dear to the prudent Cassius. He first mentions Cicero, wanting to know how he had reacted to the attempt to crown Caesar; he suggests that he be asked to join the conspiracy; he is the only one who appears moved by his death.

I do not propose to enter into the thorny question of Shakespeare's classical learning, but there is much in *Julius Caesar* to suggest that he was affected by Cicero in his way of seeing the crisis and perhaps even in his views on Stoicism and Epicureanism. A perusal of the letters and the *Philippics* will illumine one side of Shakespeare's understanding of the whole Roman crisis. The manly and frank desperation of these noble men deprived of their birthright shines through every page. Shakespeare ultimately puts the whole problem in an even larger context, but his rebellious Romans bear a strong resemblance to those we live with in Cicero's writings. Cicero was for the policies Cassius was for and doubted the wisdom both of sparing Antony and letting him speak. He disagreed with Brutus over style and apropos of him said: "no one, whether poet or orator, ever yet thought anyone else better than himself" (*Letters to Atticus* XIV. 20. May 11, 44 B.C.). Philosophically, he was neither Stoic nor Epicurean and had pointed to the difficulties in each, although he admired much in Stoicism. This seems to coincide with Shakespeare's views, and Shakespeare presents him to us as just such a middle way. The philosophical significance of his appearance in the storm can hardly be overrated. The meaning of the movements and disturbances of the heavens was a central theme of classical philosophy, and the disposition of that question went a long way in settling the human questions. Shakespeare understands this perfectly; philosophy cannot be presented on the stage, but it can be hinted at. This momentary view of Cicero and the consequences of his thought in the realities of human action could not be a central theme; but it reflects that thought with precision and indicates the weaknesses of the conspirators.

Concerning a speech of Brutus, Caesar writes Atticus:

It is, I may add, a speech of the utmost finish as far as sentiments are concerned, and in point of language not to be surpassed. Nevertheless, if I had had to handle that cause, I should have written with more fire. But the theme and the character of the writer being as you see, I was unable to correct it. For, granting the kind of orator that our Brutus aims at being, and the opinion he entertains of the best style of speech, he has secured an unqualified success. Nothing could be more finished. But I have always aimed, rightly or wrongly, at something different. However, read the speech yourself, unless indeed you have read it already, and tell me what you think of it. However, I fear that, misled by your surname, you will be somewhat hyper-Attic in your criticism. But if you will only recall Demosthenes' thunder, you will understand that the most vigorous denunciation is consistent with the purest Attic style (*ibid.*, xv. 1a. May 18, 44 B.C.).

This sounds like a critique of the funeral oration of Shakespeare's Brutus.

The "honorable men," of Antony's oration seems to come from *Philippic* II. xii. 30-31, where Cicero says that this is the way Antony spoke of the conspirators. The following statement from the same Ciceronian oration is as excellent a summary of Shakespeare's Caesar as can be found:

> In [Caesar] there was genius, reason, memory, letters, industry, thought, diligence; he had done in war things, however calamitous to the republic, yet at least great; having for many years meditated being a king, he had by great labor, great dangers, achieved what he planned; by shows, buildings, largesses, banquets he had conciliated the ignorant multitude; his followers he had bound to him by rewards, his adversaries by a show of clemency. In brief, he had already brought to a free state—partly by fear, partly by endurance—a habit of servitude (xlvii. 6.).

⁴³ IV. ii-iii. 270.

⁴⁴ IV. iii. 140-155; III. iii; I. ii. 223. Plutarch (*Brutus, op. cit.*, pp. 462-463) tells the story, but Shakespeare makes him into a poet. Shakespeare takes over Line 148 from North with only a slight change, and the original Plutarch is a quotation from Homer *Iliad* I. 259; it is from the speech of Nestor trying to reconcile Agamemnon and Achilles.

For a contrary interpretation of this passage, cf. Nietzsche, *Fröhliche Wissenschaft*, 98 (Munich: Hanser Verlag), pp. 102-103. Nietzsche believes that Shakespeare finds no fault with Brutus and asserts that this passage shows the superiority of morality to poetry and of Brutus to Shakespeare. I believe that it is intended to show exactly the opposite, and, if this is correct, the difference between Shakespeare and Nietzsche is as good a sign as could be found of the distance between the philosophic and poetic transcendence of action to be learned from Shakespeare and the modern doctrine of commitment. Nietzsche believes that Brutus is free because he acts according to his principles without fail, because he will even slay his best friend for the sake of his independence. Shakespeare teaches that he does not know the only source of freedom, a source the existence of which Nietzsche denies. Cp. Chapter 2, *supra*, pp. 30-31.

⁴⁵ IV. iii. 205-225; II. i. 13-38, 132-134. Brutus uses the same kind of ruse in trying to find out whether his servants have also seen the ghost; IV. iii. 334-357. The double announcement of Portia's death has been a subject of considerable dispute, and many editors have rejected it as an interpolation by another hand or as an oversight left by Shakespeare from an earlier draft. I can see no ground for this rejection other than that it contradicts the editors' views of Brutus' character or that they see no need for two announcements of Portia's death. This is hardly sufficient. Those passages at which our tastes most stick are perhaps most revealing of what we do not know and need to learn. For a history of the controversy, cf. the Furness variorum, *op. cit.*, pp. 222-225, and Warren D. Smith, "The Duplicate Revelation of Portia's Death," *Shakespeare Quarterly*, IV (1953), 153-161.

⁴⁶ V. i. 108-136. The suicides in the Roman plays present a peculiarly

Roman phenomenon; these heroes always had their fates in their own hands, and they were hence free; this indifference before death saved them from ever having to live slavish lives. Brutus thought himself free in an even higher sense, but here he returns to Romanness. It is impossible to care about Caesar's realm and at the same time to say that what counts in life has nothing to do with success or failure in that realm. Brutus is always somehow between the two positions—sometimes true to politics, sometimes to his philosophy. In the end, both Brutus and Cassius are too quickly disheartened and commit suicide too hastily.

47 Lessing states an opinion of Cicero's Stoic writings which formulates the problem of Brutus' morality:

I confess, I care little for Cicero's philosophy in general, and least of all for that portion of it which he displays in the second Book of his Tusculan Disputations, on the endurance of bodily pain. One would think that he wanted to train a gladiator, so eagerly does he oppose all external expression of suffering. This betokens to him, apparently, nothing more than a want of patience, nor does he seem to consider that it is often anything but voluntary, while true bravery shows itself only in voluntary actions. He only hears the cries and shrieks of Sophocles' Philoctetes, and entirely overlooks his other resolute qualities. How else would he have had the opportunity of making his rhetorical onslaught upon the poets? "They would make us effeminate by introducing the bravest men weeping." They must let them weep; for a theatre is not an arena. It behooved the condemned or mercenary combatant to do and suffer everything with propriety. Not a sound of complaint must escape his lips, not a convulsive start reveal pain. His wounds, and even his death were intended to afford delight to the spectators, and he therefore had to learn the art of entirely concealing his feelings. The slightest display of them would have awakened compassion, and compassion, if frequently excited, would soon have made an end of these cold and cruel spectacles. Now the very effect which was there avoided, the tragic stage has for its principle aim, and here, therefore, a directly opposite line of conduct is demanded. Its heroes must display their feelings, must give utterance to their pain, and let nature follow her ordinary course within them. If they betray any signs of training and forced effort, they fail to reach our hearts; and prize fighters in the *cothurnus* can at most but excite our wonder. This epithet may be applied to all the characters in the so-called tragedies of Seneca, and I am firmly convinced that the gladiatorial contests formed the principal cause why the Romans remained so far below mediocrity in the tragic art. The spectators learned, in the bloody amphitheatre, to misconceive all that is natural. . . . Philoctetes' sorrows are those of a man, but the actions those of a hero. Together they make the human hero, who is neither weak nor yet obdurate, but rather appears now the former, now the latter, according as nature or his principles of duty may require. (*Laocoön* IV. 4).

A Stoic can never appear on the stage and earn sympathy; Brutus touches only when we realize that he is not a Stoic, but he believes himself to be what he is not. In the characterization of the complementary virtues of Brutus and Cassius and the conflicts between these virtues, one is reminded of Machiavelli's teaching about the virtues a prince must possess; *Prince* xv-xix.

[48] V. i. 85-102.

[49] V. iii. 23-39; I. ii. 232; iii. 45-48. In Plutarch, Cassius explains the Epicurean depreciation of the senses and omens to Brutus (*Brutus, op. cit.*, pp. 464-465).

[50] III. i. 128-136.

5

The Limits of Politics

✑ *KING LEAR*, ACT I, SCENE i ᢒ

By Harry V. Jaffa

I

ACCORDING TO that profound student of Shakespeare, Abraham Lincoln, the most difficult task of statesmanship is that of providing, not for the foundation, but for the perpetuation, of political institutions.[1] If the political institutions are the best, to perpetuate them is not only the most difficult, but also the greatest of all the tasks of the statesman.

It is generally agreed that Shakespeare regarded monarchy as the best form of government. It is not generally realized, however, that Lear is the greatest of Shakespeare's kings. For the moment, I submit only this evidence: the supreme object of monarchical policy in the English histories is the unification and pacification of England. Only Henry V even approaches success in this, but, in view of his questionable title to the throne, he is compelled to create a dubious national unity by means of an unjust foreign war. Yet the first scene in *King Lear* shows the old monarch at the head of a united Britain (not merely England) and at peace, not only with all domestic factions, but with the outside world as well. France and Burgundy, who represent this world, are suitors for the hand of Lear's youngest daughter. Never in the histories does Shakespeare represent his native land at such a peak of prestige and political excellence; in *King Lear* alone do we find actualized the consummation devoutly wished by all other good Shakespearean kings.

If Lear is, in fact, Shakespeare's greatest king and if it is true that to perpetuate such a rule is an even greater task than to establish it, then the opening of *King Lear* shows us the old king confronted with the supreme problem of his great career—that of providing for the succession to his throne. The action whereby he provides for this succession should, therefore, be his greatest action. Since it would be the greatest action of the greatest king and since monarchy is the best form of government, such an action would be Shakespeare's presentation of the consummation of the political art, of political virtue and therewith of political life altogether. But such a presentation could imply even more than this; for, if Shakespeare, as a Renaissance classicist, regarded man as a political animal, it is possible that he regarded the fulfillment of man's highest political function as identical to the fulfillment of his highest human function. It is not improbable, then, that the stage is set, at the opening of *King Lear,* for Shakespeare's presentation of the ultimate in human existence.

II

The foregoing will, no doubt, strike many as paradoxical. That *King Lear* contains the fullest demonstration of Shakespeare's creative powers and that these somehow represent the ultimate in man's humanity is a proposition that would be widely concurred in. Yet I believe that this latter proposition is consistent with, if not identical to, the former ones. For, if Shakespeare undertook the fullest revelation of his powers in *King Lear,* then it is entirely probable that the story of the play was selected as the most suitable vehicle for this revelation. In other words, the question why we find in *King Lear* the fullest revelation of Shakespeare's genius may be identical to the question, Why does Shakespeare reveal himself to us most fully in a play in which his greatest king is confronted with the task of perpetuating the perfect political regime?

Although many critics have opined that *King Lear* is Shakespeare's greatest work, few call it their favorite play,[2] and few fail to remark adversely on many of its dramatic properties. I will here quote some remarks of Coleridge, who expresses, in somewhat exaggerated form, perhaps, assumptions which have characterized a great deal of the critical literature dealing with the play in the nineteenth and twentieth centuries. Although Coleridge has been attacked on many grounds by recent critics, I do not believe that these particular assumptions have been sufficiently challenged. As will readily appear, they imply a general conception as to the meaning of the play—a meaning which is, in my judgment, inconsistent with the high estimate in which the play is otherwise held. According to Coleridge, one can "Omit the first scene in *Lear,* and everything will remain"; the first scene is a "nursery tale," "prefixed as the *porch* of the edifice, not laid as its foundation."[3] In *King Lear,* says Coleridge, "the interest and situations . . . are derived from a gross improbability."[4] This is but an application of Coleridge's principle that, in a Shakespearean play, the interest does not derive from, indeed is independent of, interest in plot and story. "Shakespeare did not take the trouble of inventing stories. It was enough for him to select from those that had been invented or recorded such as had one or other, or both, of two recommendations, namely, suitableness to his purposes, and second, their being already parts of popular tradition. . . ."[5] Coleridge thus implies that it was less trouble for Shakespeare to take over tales already told than to invent new ones. Yet, since Coleridge admits that Shakespeare had a purpose in writing a play distinct from that of evoking response to the familiar, his choosing only from the available stock of traditional materials must have imposed greater restrictions on him than if he had felt free to go outside that stock. There certainly is no assurance that Shakespeare was saving himself trouble because he did not invent stories. That he was neither lazy nor indifferent in his attitude toward his stories is obvious from the fact that he frequently and freely altered his source materials. There is, certainly, no a priori reason for assuming that the adaptation of plot and story to Shakespeare's purpose in writing a play were not so deliberate and extensive as in his handling of any other of his materials.

From the view that the story of *King Lear* is an absurd fairy tale, Coleridge infers that none of the action initiated by Lear in Scene i is to be taken seriously. Yet Coleridge does not fail to observe one fact inconsistent with this general thesis: "It was not without forethought, and it is not without its due significance, that the triple division is stated here (I. i. 1-6) as already determined and in all its particulars, previously to the trial of professions, as the relative rewards of which the daughters were to be made to consider their several portions." [6] A. C. Bradley, commenting on this observation, says that the love test is a "mere form, devised as a childish scheme to gratify his love of absolute power and his hunger for assurances of devotion." Yet neither Coleridge nor Bradley has reflected on the possibility that, if the love test, the trick whereby Lear makes it appear that he is "dividing his kingdom among his daughters in proportion to the strength of their protestations of love," [7] is a pretense, then perhaps much more in the scene is also pretense. Coleridge and Bradley rightly assume that to make the division of the kingdom depend on such protestations could only signify insane vanity and folly, but they also assume that Lear is doing no such thing. Why, then, do they insist that he is vain and foolish nonetheless? May not this pretense be part of a larger system of pretenses? How do we know that this alone is a pretense and nothing else? In truth, we know no such thing. Since Lear in the course of the scene does alter the division of the kingdom to fit the strength of the protestations, one may say that the previously decided division was merely tentative. If we are to maintain the view that the love test was really intended as a sham, we must base our view on other and stronger evidence.

It is impossible to drop Scene i from the play, as Coleridge suggests, for the reason given by Bradley: that "it is essential that Lear's contribution to the action of the drama . . . be remembered; not at all that we may feel that he 'deserved' what he suffered, but because otherwise his fate would appear to us at best pathetic, at worst shocking, but certainly not tragic."[8] It is then equally impossible to impute to Lear a serious intention to make the division of the kingdom depend on his daughters' protestations, since we would thus be forced to regard him as already insane, not morally responsible, and accordingly unable to contribute in any moral or dramatic sense to the action of the play. It would seem that the only tenable hypothesis is that the love test was, from its beginning, a pretense.

But, if Lear's sanity and, with it, his status as a tragic hero depends on the premise that the love test is a pretense, then the whole meaning of the play, i.e., the meaning of Lear's suffering, depends on our making this hypothesis intelligible. We do not know why he must suffer if we do not know why he adopted the pretense which was the efficient cause of that suffering.

The generally accepted explanation is that of Bradley: Lear is a foolish, vain, selfish old man whose wits are beginning to fail. His failings are extenuated by his "long life of absolute power, in which he has been flattered to the top of his bent" and which "has produced in him that blindness to human limitations, and the presumptuous self-will, which in Greek tragedy we have so often seen stumbling against the altar of Nemesis." Yet this extenuation, besides being contradicted by internal evidence—which I shall present shortly—runs athwart the larger bias of the play, for it is widely admitted that the sufferings of Lear are the most terrible in all Shakespeare and, probably, a fortiori, in the whole of the world's literature. But great passion, be it that of Lear, of Oedipus, or of Jesus, implies greatness in the soul of the sufferer. A great passion is always, in some sense, compensation for a great error. As Plato teaches in the *Republic*, great errors are the work of great souls, souls capable of either great good or great evil. A petty soul is one that can accomplish neither great good nor great evil. It seems impossible to suppose that a child, a fool, or a knave would be capable of the passion of a Lear. Is it not, then, as impossible to suppose that the error which was, in an important way, the cause of such a passion was childish, foolish, or knavish? It is true that the action which precipitated Lear's passion was a sign of the absence of perfect wisdom. But it seems to me that no consistent view of the play as a whole is possible that does not account for

Lear's unwisdom Scene i as a defect such as only the very greatest soul could suffer. Bradley's explanation of Lear's failure in Scene i is, I think, clearly deficient, in that it is at least compatible with the view that Lear's error was the error of a petty soul.

III

I have suggested that the stage is set at the beginning of the play for the supreme action of Lear's long and successful reign, the action whereby he provides for its perpetuation. The consciousness of critics has, I believe, been so dominated by Lear's apparent failure in this scene that they have failed to notice his serious intention. Yet the meaning and extent of Lear's failure can be grasped with precision only in the light of his intentions. We must then try to understand exactly how Lear undertook to solve this paramount political problem. Coleridge, it will be remembered, inferred (rightly, I believe) from Gloucester's first speech that Lear's division of the kingdom was determined "in all its particulars"; but Coleridge says no more about these particulars. Bradley, however, observes that it "seems to have escaped the attention of Coleridge and others" [9] that Lear's original plan was not so absurd as it has been taken to be. For example, Lear never intended to live with his three daughters in turn, but with Cordelia alone. He then concludes that Lear's

> . . . whole original plan, though foolish and rash, was not a "hideous rashness" or incredible folly. If carried out it would have had no such consequences as followed its alteration. It would probably have led quickly to war, but not to the agony which culminated in the storm upon the heath.

Bradley calls our attention to the fact that catastrophe is the consequence, not of Lear's original plan, but of the alteration of that plan. Bradley assumes, without any attempt at proof, that Lear's original plan was also foolish and rash, although not "hideously rash." In a footnote to the latter phrase, he mentions that it is Kent who applies this epithet to the *altered* plan. Yet Bradley does not attempt the possible inference that, if Kent, within the play, was informed concerning the original plan "in all its particulars" and had expressed no objection to it, then perhaps he had approved of it. This is, in fact, a necessary inference, if we are not to suppose that Kent, who does not even express a private doubt to his fellow-councilor Gloucester was, until the penultimate moment of his public service, a time-serving flatterer. But, if the original plan had Kent's and Gloucester's approval, it may not have been foolish at all. It may, indeed, have been a product of sound principles of statecraft.

The proposition that Kent and Gloucester approved Lear's original plan is a necessary inference for anyone who does not reject the premise that, in general, the relationship of characters in a Shakespearean play is made to appear to flow from their entire lives and not to start up, *de novo*, with the raising of the curtain. Lear, Kent, Gloucester, and the three daughters are supposed to have known one another and to have lived in intimate association for many years. Kent is the King's favorite courtier, as Cordelia is his favorite daughter. Both Kent and Cordelia are, in similar ways, mirrors of the master and father they love. Bradley's statement that Lear has been corrupted by flattery and has a foolish craving for it is contradicted by the fact that Lear prefers above all others the two people in the play who are represented as absolutely incapable of flattery or hypocrisy. We can no more suppose that Kent and Cordelia are blunt and plain-spoken to the King for the first time (or that he loved them for anything but their true qualities) than that they have been petty flatterers until the moment the action of the play begins. The long-standing difference between Cordelia and her sisters is stressed in her farewell to them, and they themselves emphasize their father's preference for Cordelia. Moreover, Lear's preference for Cordelia and Kent is consistent with a widely recognized principle of the soul: the principle that self-love is the basis of friendship and that we prefer as friends those who are most like ourselves.[10] Lear's own nature is not that of a flatterer, and, hence, we would expect him to prefer those who were not flatterers. Lear's political success, moreover, would be difficult to understand if he did not have about him those who would tell him the truth. The truth about Lear himself may be said to be "flattering," in the

sense that Lear was an honest and noble-hearted man and evoked the spontaneous loyalty and devotion of such a man as Kent. There are few, if any, characters in Shakespeare who command such unqualified esteem as Kent; yet Kent's life is constituted by his devotion to Lear. But, if Lear were not worthy of this devotion, if, that is to say, Kent's discrimination in choosing an object of devotion were questionable, however unselfish the devotion itself, our admiration for Kent would assuredly be mingled with either pity or contempt. That we do not feel the least pity or contempt for Kent is, I think, a sign of Lear's, as well as of Kent's, true worth.

If Kent knew Lear's original plan in all its particulars, he must have approved it, since he is silent concerning any defects it may have possessed and since we know that he did not hesitate to protest in the most vehement manner when Lear departed from it. If it be objected that Kent may have disapproved the original plan but acceded to it after he had exhausted his influence in having it rectified, there is this reply: someone as loyal and devoted as Kent would surely have been preoccupied with the danger to his master, had he anticipated any. Yet, in the moment before the stage fills with the court, we see him and Gloucester turn lightly from state to personal matters, without any sign of apprehension concerning the former. What, then, was the original plan?

I V

The negative view that Bradley and others have taken of the original plan has centered, as has been said, on the love test. The love test has already been dismissed as a pretense, as far as the original division of the kingdom is concerned. The real objection has always been to the division of the kingdom itself. It has always been thought that, since the supreme object of monarchical policy in Shakespeare is the unification of England, a British king who deliberately divides a united kingdom is committing the supreme act of monarchical folly.

Yet, reflection must make us cautious of accepting this view. First of all, there looms the paradox of imputing the crime of dividing the kingdom to the one Shakespearean king whose ascendancy appears to have united it—a paradox enforced by Kent's apparent acquiescence. Second is the radical difference between dividing the kingdom into two, as distinct from three. The very number two is, traditionally, the number for strife, as the number three is the number for unity. Without pursuing allegorical possibilities, it is clear that a balance of power can be better preserved where there are three distinct forces, no one of which can overmatch the other two, than where there are only two forces, however evenly matched. The most important reflection, however, concerns whether, in dividing the kingdom, Lear was doing, during his lifetime, what in any event was bound to come to pass after his death. That is, how do we know that the unity achieved by Lear was not itself the result of an equipoise of forces, in unstable equilibrium, rather than a simple unity? In order to understand Lear's policy, one must analyze the problem he faced, the problem of the succession, in terms of the political realities which confronted him.

We must observe that Lear's problem is complicated by the fact that he had three daughters but no son. Yet, if Lear had had a son the difficulty would not have been greatly different. Lear would still have had to gain the support of major powers in the kingdom—and abroad—for his settlement. And he had to bind them to that settlement by both pledges and self-interest in order to assure its durability. It is striking that, although Goneril and Regan have been married for some time, they have not yet received dowries.[11] All three daughters must receive their dowries simultaneously. Does this fact not indicate that Lear was thinking in terms of an over-all balance of power, each part of which was needed to ensure the rest? Had Lear's power been as absolute as it has seemed, why should he have hesitated so long to give the elder daughters their dowries? Lear was certainly using the dowries and the marriages as instruments of policy, as was the custom in royal (and not only royal) houses. Burgundy and France have "long" made their amorous sojourn at his court, and presumably it is much longer since Cornwall and Albany first made theirs. Lear has delayed as long as possible making his final disposition of both the hands and fortunes of his daughters. What, then, was Lear's matrimonial policy?

First, we must note that Cornwall and Albany represent the geographical extremities of Britain. Cornwall clearly represents the south. Albany, according to Holinshed, originally was the northern part of the island and included Scotland. At I. iv. 179, the Fool tells Lear: "Thou hast pared thy wit o' both sides, and left nothing i' the middle," indicating that the two extremities (Goneril and Regan) have digested the center portion, which was to have been Cordelia's. Lear had married his two older daughters to two great lords whose estates (and, hence, we may assume, whose power) lay at the opposite poles of the kingdom. Now, anyone who knows only as much of English history as is contained in Shakespeare's histories knows that English kings found it impossible to exercise control in any region very remote from the center of the royal domains without the support of the feudal potentates of those regions.[12] The selection of sons-in-law from the remote portions of his kingdom indicates, I believe, that Lear's unification of the kingdom was in part due to his ability to secure the adhesion of the lords of these outlying districts through marriage to the royal house. But the marriage of a daughter involves a dowry; Cornwall and Albany expected more than brides, and the possibility that a descendant might occupy the throne. What could be more natural than that they expected lands that lay in the neighborhoods of their ancestral estates?

From this it would seem that Lear's action in dividing the kingdom was not arbitrary or foolish; it was an action predestined by the very means required to bring unity to the kingdom. Lear, it appears, delayed the division as long as possible, but he could not put it off indefinitely, any more than he could put off indefinitely his own demise.

In Lear's speech announcing to the court the division of the kingdom into three parts, he gives two reasons for his action: first, that he wishes to shake all care and business from his age, conferring them on younger strengths; and, second, "that future strife may be prevented now." There is a sense in which these two reasons may be regarded as a single one; that is, by devising a political arrangement whereby the peace of the kingdom could be ensured without the adventitious factor of his personal ascendancy, Lear removed his chief present care by providing against future strife. However, if we view these two reasons more superficially, I think that it would be correct to say that the second reason is the real one and the first primarily an excuse for the latter. It is difficult to believe that failing strength was a pressing motive for Lear's action; the old man was the most prodigious octogenarian on record, still spending his days hunting, and able, as the last act shows, to kill a man single-handed.

The decisive consideration, however, is this: there is no evidence that, in the original plan, Lear intended anything resembling an abdication. On the contrary is the fact that Lear never abandoned the crown. What he divided between his sons-in-law, in the flush of his rage against Cordelia, was a coronet.[13] He himself was to retain, even in the altered plan, "The name, and all th' additions to a king." Yet, as long as Lear retained the name of king, a name which he in no way shared with a successor, his delegation of authority to his sons-in-law remained fundamentally distinguished from an abdication.[14] One may ask why Lear held a coronet in his hand at all. The answer is, I believe, that the coronet, the symbol of ducal authority, was intended for Cordelia's husband.[15] It must be remembered that the scene was intended to be one in which Cordelia received her husband and dowry. Her husband, whether Burgundy or France, would be a foreigner, whose British dukedom would be conferred along with Cordelia's hand. To sum up: Lear might have delegated much of his "business" to his sons-in-law in the original plan, but there is no sign of anything resembling an abdication. As long as he did not abdicate, he would, as king, remain the only personage capable of deciding the highest political questions. Since there is no explicit mention, anywhere in the scene, of a successor, the implication is left that Lear would retain the power of naming a successor, and this in turn indicates an intention to retain decisive power.

Lear's original plan called, I think, for precisely equal shares to go to Albany and Cornwall, husbands of the two older daughters. But Cordelia was to receive a third "more opulent" than the other two. Lear divided his kingdom into "three," but the parts are not mathematical "thirds." Cordelia was not only to be situated in the middle, but to have the richest portion of the realm. Lear, as Bradley pointed out, intended to live with Cordelia alone. Living on as king with Cordelia, with Albany and Cornwall acting as his deputies in regions which he could not control without their loyalty anyway, does it seem that Lear was giving up anything that he could in any case have kept to himself much longer? Since Cordelia's husband would be a foreigner, living in the midst of Lear's long-time retainers, it is difficult to imagine any such conflict of domestic authority arising, as a result of the original plan, as arose in the altered plan. In the altered plan, the division of Cordelia's inheritance between Goneril and Regan left Lear's original retainers a minority among those owing primary fealty to Albany and Cornwall. But, in the original plan, any retainers the husband of Cordelia brought with him to England would in all likelihood have remained a small minority in comparison to those who had been brought up to regard Lear as their master. All indications within the play are that Lear evoked the strongest loyalty from those who recognized him as their legitimate master.

Concerning the marriage of Cordelia, I think the evidence is overwhelming in favor of the view that she was intended as the bride of Burgundy. First, because Lear offers her to Burgundy, although this is after her disinheritance.[16] Second, because Burgundy has had previous knowledge of Cordelia's dowry. But such knowledge implies at the same time that he has been privy to some, if not all, of Lear's intended scheme. Such a confidential position certainly suggests the status of an intended son-in-law. Now, France and Burgundy were traditional enemies. Their presence at Lear's court suggests that Cordelia's dowry would have been an important counter in the balance of power between them.[17] Burgundy is the lesser power, as is shown by Lear's style in addressing him and by the fact that Lear fears insulting France, but not Burgundy. Cordelia's marriage to France would have been a political blunder of the first magnitude, a blunder of which there is no reason to suspect the Lear who drafted the plan approved by Kent and Gloucester. A French marriage would inevitably have given rise to the French claims to the British throne, such as actually led to the French invasion that occurs in the play. Lear would never have intended, nor would Kent have consented, that the King of France or his descendants inherit the throne of Britain. In such a case, there would have been the possibility, at least, that Britain would become the appendage of France. Moreover, such a marriage would have heavily unbalanced the system of powers, as that system is envisaged within the horizon of the play. France, commanding the fairest part of Britain, might easily have overmatched Burgundy, thereafter to hold the remainder of Britain in his power. On the other hand, however, Cordelia's dowry, added to Burgundy, might have aided the balance of power on the Continent.[18] Conversely, Burgundy, added to Cordelia's part of Britain, would have neutralized any combination of the older sisters. A combination of the powers of Albany and Cornwall with France against Cordelia and Burgundy, even apart from its geographical difficulty, would have been unlikely. The victory of Goneril and Regan over Cordelia, if achieved with the aid of France, would in all likelihood leave the elder sisters at the mercy of their great ally, to be overpowered and absorbed in turn. We may, however, ask why France, who was no doubt a political reasoner, wasted his time in a vain suit at Lear's court? The answer is, I think, in the first place, that the marriage was too important for him to be absent from the scene of its negotiation. We must remember that Goneril and Regan must have had an intense interest, not only in their younger sister's dowry, but in her marriage. The moment of Cordelia's betrothal to Burgundy would be the precise moment for France to cultivate good relations with her older sisters. There remained, however, as a remote possibility, what actually came to pass. Just as the first Queen Elizabeth could always flirt with French dukes as a threat to Spain, so could Lear use a French marriage for Cordelia as a threat to Goneril, Regan, and their husbands, should they fail to acquiesce in the preferred treatment given Cordelia in the division of the kingdom.

Although the basic problem facing Lear was that of the succession to the throne, there is no direct reference in the text to the subject of a prospective heir. If Cordelia were married to Burgundy, however, it would seem probable that the crown was intended to pass to Cordelia and her descendants. Burgundy would be elevated in the feudal hierarchy by his marriage to a king's daughter, and his ancestral dukedom might become an appendage to the kingdom of Britain, rather than the reverse. Elements in the English tradition would seem to confirm the soundness of this view. The ascent of a foreign duke, William of Normandy, to the throne of England gave English kings claims on the French throne, but not the reverse. Also, the marriage of Mary Tudor to Philip II was a "Burgundian" marriage. It was unhappy and politically near-disastrous, but principally because of the difficulties flowing from the Reformation. No such religious questions are envisaged within the play's horizon. The relevant point is that Mary, although married to a foreign prince who was nominally king of England, alone exercised the powers of the sovereign. Philip was never more than the consort of the queen, even though he was heir to a throne in his own right. A Burgundian marriage, in short, would have made the succession of Cordelia to the throne a viable political arrangement. Lear's scheme of marrying Cordelia to Burgundy gave good promise of leading to a stable international system and a peaceful acceptance of Lear's will and testament at home.

It is not clear whether Lear intended to make an announcement concerning the succession at the court we witness in Scene i. In my judgment, he did not intend to do so. It would have been apparent to everyone, from the preferred treatment of Cordelia, that he intended the crown to pass to her. Yet the precise terms of the inheritance of the crown itself would have left some scope for diplomacy. The absence of evidence on which to decide what these terms might have been suggests that Lear himself was not yet in a position to fix them. The evidence I have cited suggests that Lear, being truly wise in the ways of politics, was not a man to force premature decisions and that he was in no hurry to give up any more of his authority than necessary. But the announcement of the succession would have involved some further sacrifice of authority. Like any outgoing officeholder, Lear's authority would be diminished the moment his successor was known. Those who would be reluctant to oppose the king openly, as long as they had hopes of influencing him in their favor, would lose some of that reluctance the moment they were certain that his decision was against them. The succession of Cordelia to the throne had to be accomplished in a succession of steps, each of which required something of a pause in order to test its firmness. The first step was to be the granting of the dowries, simultaneously with the announcement of the marriage. Why these had to be done in one step has been indicated; only in virtue of a foreign marriage, in which a foreign force would be united to Cordelia's native strength, could she defend her inheritance from her sisters. The realignment of power resulting from the dowries and the marriage would be the essential basis of the future succession. But in a feudal system, in which power depended heavily on personal loyalties, public pledges would not be a negligible factor in guaranteeing the success of Lear's arrangements.[19] How to secure those pledges was a consideration prior to any plan to announce the succession itself. In my judgment, the love test was, in one of its meanings, a part of Lear's deliberate system of policy. Its purpose was to supply, at least inferentially, pledges of support for the division of the kingdom which he was in process of announcing. As I shall shortly demonstrate, these pledges were demanded only from Goneril and Regan, not from Cordelia. They were, that is, demanded only from those who might have motives to repudiate his division.

Certainly, Lear did not have any practical doubt concerning the nature of his daughters' love for him. He had already arranged things to favor Cordelia as much as possible. Not only was the kingdom divided on the map before the start of the court scene, but Lear gave Goneril and then Regan their shares after each had spoken, without hearing the other. Thus, Cordelia's "more opulent" third was awaiting her, as the remainder, before she spoke a word. Clearly, Lear's intention was not to weigh the speeches against the shares in any manner or sense. Yet his shrewd knowledge of his elder daughters put them in a position in which it would have been ludicrous for them to repudiate their father's judgment after their fulsome speeches of devotion.

We do not know whether Kent, Gloucester, Burgundy, or anyone else knew of the king's plan to administer the test. There was great need for secrecy. Many commentators have noted that Goneril and Regan were taken by surprise. It was absolutely necessary that they should have been. If they had had any inkling of the test, they would have sought means other than protestations to increase their bargaining power.[20] They would have quickly guessed that speeches could give them no advantage, that the advantage already lay with Cordelia.[21] The least they might have done was to boycott the court. Had they done this, for however specious a reason, they could have held up the settlements. If these were made in their absence and in the teeth of their objections, they might have challenged the legitimacy of their father's will. Thus, their power to absent themselves from the court might itself have become a bargaining counter, with which they might have exacted a forfeit. The love test, taking them by surprise, trapped them into professions which they otherwise might never have made. Commentators have long noted the swiftness of the action in Scene i,[22] and, in the case of the love test, have taken it as additional evidence of Lear's rashness. Yet a sufficient reason for Lear's haste would be his anxiety to have his plan consummated before Goneril and Regan could recover poise enough to object to it. Lear's very haste may be regarded as craftiness. We know that the professions were not intended to determine the shares, but Goneril and Regan could not know that. As far as Goneril knew, her fortune might depend on the effect of her speech. Regan may have suspected that this was not the case, but, with more than two-thirds of the kingdom remaining, she would take no chance. Cordelia alone of the three, seeing the remainder plainly before her on the map, knew in advance precisely what her share was to be. Cordelia alone, therefore, knew that her speech was not needed to establish her share. To Cordelia, it must have been apparent that the test was a trick devised in her interest and that Lear, far from demanding that she heave her heart into her mouth, was making his own protestation of love to her. In truth, Lear was not asking Cordelia to flatter him. Lear rightly counted on the hypocrisy of the elder daughters betraying them. But, when he turns to Cordelia, he seems rather to say, "See how I have turned their greed against them and reserved the fairest portion for you, whose love I have never doubted."

V

This analysis is now exposed to a grave objection. If Lear has, all along, judged correctly the characters of his daughters, as I have maintained, and, if the love test is meant to exploit the hypocrisy of Goneril and Regan in the interest of Cordelia's truth, why does Lear react so violently to that very truth? If his affection for Cordelia is due to the very qualities she here displays in so transcendent a manner, why, then, does he not place the same interpretation on her behavior that Kent does and that we do and tell the court that he sees in her blunt refusal to compete with her sisters the virtue that he all along wished to reward with the greatest share? Would not this have been hailed as a vindication of the old King's judgment, just as Bassanio's choice of the leaden casket vindicated the judgment of Portia's father in *The Merchant of Venice*?

The answer to this difficulty must be in terms both of the conscious motivation which we can ascribe to Lear and of an unconscious motivation. Before attempting this analysis of motives, however, it is desirable to restate the general thesis maintained concerning the play as a whole. I have said that the subject of the play is monarchy and that it represents the supreme action of the greatest king. The first and most obvious objection to this thesis was the assertion that the king we see in action in Scene i is a foolish, vain old man and not a great king at all. Our reconstruction of Lear's statecraft should make it possible now to waive that objection. But the subsequent apparent failure of that statecraft, far from refuting the claims concerning its merits, is actually necessary in order to vindicate those claims.

In order that Shakespeare may make us understand what the greatest action of the greatest king is, it is necessary that he present us with an action that "fails." If the action succeeded, we could not identify it as the greatest action, for then we could not know that the difficulty of the action was such as to require the utmost in human virtue. In determining the tensile strength of a cord, it is necessary to find the least weight that will *break* the cord in order to find the greatest weight the cord will support. So it was necessary for Shakespeare to show us the point at which the most skillful policy of his most successful king *broke* in order to point out, and thus define for us, the limits of kingly virtue. And if, as suggested above, Shakespeare regarded kingly virtue as the highest human virtue, he would thereby mark out for us the limits of human life, distinguishing it both from the life that is more than human and from the life that is less than human.[23]

Let us return now to our difficulty. In brief, it is my thesis that Lear is, on the conscious level, outraged by the injustice of Cordelia's refusal to permit the consummation of his carefully contrived plan. But the violence of his outrage is due to an unconscious sense that that very consummation, which he thinks he desired, would have violated and forever frustrated a passion far more profound than the passion for political success. For Lear, in striking at Cordelia, strikes also at his own handiwork. To understand the violence of Lear's eruption, we must understand the unconscious necessity he was under to destroy that political edifice which it had been his life's work to construct.

Starting from Lear's conscious motivation, we can answer the objection we have posed by observing that Lear certainly did not want the love test to *appear* as a trick. To have done so would have run counter to a host of the political considerations we have advanced. Albany and Cornwall were not to be insulted. Lear wanted the entire scene to be a public "love feast." In this, Lear was acting the role of a hypocrite, we might say, but his hypocrisy was only a concession to his sense of justice. He had devised the best plan for the kingdom, for the common good, and any compromise that he had made with truth was made for the sake of justice. Cordelia's uncompromising, intransigent truthfulness contrasted, then, with his own willingness to sacrifice for the common good.[24] If we remember the key part that Cordelia was to play in the entire plan, we can begin to understand the sense of outrage, even betrayal, that the old man must have felt.

Although the mere fact of Lear's rage can be accounted for by this surface explanation, its violence and its tragic consequences are intelligible only if we relate what occurred on the surface to what occurred beneath it. What occurred beneath the surface may be summarized by saying that, when Cordelia jarred her father by her unexpected response, she upset not only his political plan, but his personal plan, which was to express his love of Cordelia. We must grasp the nature of Lear's need to express this love if we are to understand the passion loosed when that need was frustrated.

Let us turn again to the love test, a dramatic device brilliantly adapted to Shakespeare's multiple purpose in Scene i. Its function on the level of mere policy has been sketched.

Lear asks his daughters to tell him how much they love him. In effect, he commands their love. Yet, love cannot be commanded; only professions of love can be. By the love test, Shakespeare establishes one precise limit of Lear's power to command and, thereby, one limit of kingly power and virtue. But Lear asks his daughters to tell him how much they love him that he may proportion his bounty to their merit. He thus proclaims a kingly desire to proceed on the rules of distributive justice while also implying that love for himself is a proper test of merit in others. This latter implication is not mere vanity, if Lear is the great ruler we have said he is, for the daughter who loves him most will in all likelihood be the most meritorious, since she will most nearly resemble her father.[25] Yet, in proclaiming his desire to make a just distribution, Lear tacitly admits the necessity he is under to know the truth concerning his daughters' love for him. But what the love test discloses is the impossibility that Lear can ever have such knowledge as long as he remains on his throne.

If it is true that love cannot be commanded, then he who possesses the power to command professions of love must be at a particular disadvantage in distinguishing genuine from spurious manifestations of love. Because Lear could, as king, command professions of love, it was impossible for him ever to be certain that an expression of love for him, whether by Cordelia or another, was not in fact a response to his power of command.[26] Lear thought that Cordelia loved him most because he saw in her the reflection of his own kingliness. But, if imitation is the sincerest kind of flattery, how could Lear ever distinguish the imitation of flattery from that generated by his virtue in the souls of those who really loved him? Cordelia's defiance in the love test only brought into the open the king's essential impotence, for it is not impossible to ascribe to Cordelia a very shrewd selfishness in Scene i. Consider the consequences of her boldness: she was the intended bride of the "waterish" Burgundy; but, losing her dowry she loses a poor lover and gains a superior one, France. Not only does France exhibit a nobility of character that makes him seem worthy of his bride, but he is a king in his own right and, as we quickly learn, one who has no intention of abandoning his bride's claims.[27] Accordingly, Cordelia's course could be interpreted, not only as a sacrifice of public interest to private happiness, but as a clever scheme to become queen of France and England, thus defeating Lear's just policy, which is national and patriotic. Goneril and Regan were shallow hypocrites; but how could Lear know that Cordelia was not a clever one?

Lear, I have said, implies that love of himself is a test of merit in others. To assume the validity of such a test is, we might say, of the essence of monarchy. Love of justice, in a monarchy, is thought to be identical, in essence, to love of the monarch, because he is thought to incorporate justice.[28] Lear, I have said, is a great king. A great king must have great power, for, without such power, he would not be obeyed, and, if he were not obeyed, he would not be a great king. Lear, then, must have great power or, what comes to the same thing, the illusion of great power.[29] The root of Lear's power is the conviction, in the hearts of both king and subjects, that he is justice incarnate. Yet the absoluteness of Lear's power, founded on this conviction, shuts him off from the very knowledge on which that justice would have to be based if it were what it seems to be, for a spontaneous show of love cannot be distinguished from a clever imitation, except by a god who can search men's hearts. Humanly speaking, the power to discern disinterested motives, however limited in the best case, exists in inverse ratio to the power to command.[30] In proclaiming love of himself as the principle of distributive justice, Lear in fact proclaimed, as the basis of his justice, a godlike knowledge. Lear, we might say, is compelled by the nature of his situation to pretend to a perfection he does not possess in order to actualize a perfection he does possess.

But what meaning are we to ascribe to the expression, "perfection he does possess"? Lear, I have said, is a great ruler. The unity and amity of the kingdom, although seen for the most part retrospectively and through the attachment to him of all the "good" characters, are witness to this. Yet, granting Lear this superiority, we can still say that Lear never had more than an opinion of his own justice.[31] If we were to assume that such a regime is the best of which human life admits, we would, nonetheless, have to say that the best is, in a decisive sense, an illusion.[32] We would be further driven to conclude that Lear's greatness as a king is an illusion. Lear's supposed knowledge of his daughters' love of him, which was to have been the basis of his greatest and ostensibly most just political action, is of the essence of the illusion.

The crux of the situation is this: that the illusion which is the basis of Lear's policy, though adequate for all the purposes of political life, becomes intolerable at the decisive moment in the love test. The old king has need of genuine love. The entire scene, we must remember, is due to his mortality, to the fact that he must provide for a successor. The very insufficiency which necessitates a succession necessitates love. A god could be loved without loving, but a man cannot. If Lear possessed the perfection which, as king, he pretends to, he would be capable of being loved without loving. But Lear lacks such perfection. His need of love is radical. In pretending to the attributes of divinity, a pretense necessary to the operation of his seemingly most just rule, Lear has had to deny the claims of his humanity. As king, he has denied humanity to serve humanity.[33] Cordelia, however, by her action, destroys the possibility of consummating that self-denial.

We must now analyze the precise impact that Cordelia's refusal had on her father and attempt to comprehend the interaction of his conscious and unconscious motivation. At the moment Lear rejects Cordelia, calls her stranger, and dowers her with his curse, she has in fact become a stranger to him. For Lear, in attempting to carry out the well-contrived pretense or deception of the love test, had not hesitated to compromise with truth, albeit for the sake of justice. Cordelia, in refusing to make any such compromise, showed herself in her intransigence unlike her father. But it is this appearance of unlikeness, rather than the appearance of disobedience, that made a mockery of his plan, for the plan was founded on the assumption of such a likeness. But Lear's assumption that Cordelia loved him and that she was like him involved even more than the question of whether he was sound in his intention to make her his successor, for Lear had seen what he thought was the image of his own soul in Cordelia. His passion for Cordelia was his self-love transfigured; in his identification with her, he saw his monarchy perpetuated beyond the grave. His faith in the truth of that image caused him to place faith in the bearer of the image. But, bewildered by the sudden strangeness of the bearer, Lear could no longer recognize the image, and with this he lost the sheet anchor of what had hitherto been his existence. A colloquy in *Julius Caesar* may help to clarify what is here intended:

> CASSIUS Tell me, good Brutus, can you see your face?
> BRUTUS No, Cassius, for the eye sees not itself
> But by reflection, by some other things.
>
> . . . .
>
> CASSIUS Therefore, good Brutus, be prepared to hear.
> And since you know you cannot see yourself
> So well as by reflection, I your glass
> Will modestly discover to yourself
> That of yourself which you yet know not of.
> *Julius Caesar* I. ii. 60-82.

Lear's alienation from Cordelia involved his alienation from the basis of such self-knowledge as he believed himself to possess. He became alienated not only from her, but from himself and from the world within which he had seen himself in his own mind's eye.[34] Lear's original, conventional kingliness was intrinsic to the world implied by the image of himself which he saw reflected in Cordelia. The strange image which Cordelia now reflected separated Lear from this world, the world in which he had been king. He could not continue as king, as his original plan required, when he no longer had a basis for faith in that world. Yet some part of the passion of the outburst against Cordelia, like that against his other daughters later in the play, is due to his attachment to that lost world, an attachment not to be overcome lightly or in a moment. His attachment to justice was at the root of his attachment to that world, and the tragedy of *King Lear* lies in the necessity of Lear to abandon even his attachment to justice when the claims of love and truth are brought to bear in all their uncompromising imperiousness.

The deeper meaning of the love test was foreshadowed when we observed that Cordelia, alone of the three sisters, knew in advance of her speech what her share of the kingdom was to be. Cordelia, I said, knew that her father, far from demanding a profession of love from her, was making a profession of love to her. In the test, Lear becomes the lover, and Cordelia the beloved. But the relation of beloved to lover is that of cause to effect, of superior to inferior. When Lear, responding to Cordelia's "Nothing," tells her that nothing comes of nothing, he expresses the axiom on which all understanding of causality is founded. He tells her that there is no effect without a cause. He implies that she cannot cause him to be bountiful without obeying him. He does not know, however, that, by becoming the lover, the only bounty he has to offer is his love and that Cordelia, as beloved, can only cause his love by refusing to surrender the sovereignty which he has himself now thrust on her. Ironically, Lear is attempting to command Cordelia at precisely the moment and in the very situation in which his relation to her has been reversed, and she has become the commanding one, for, when Lear turned to Cordelia to hear her profession, she had already ascended a throne. It was not the throne of Britain, but rather the invisible throne prepared by nature for those of surpassing virtue.

We have noted above that Lear's choice of Cordelia as his successor was based on a translegal conception of political right, in that he did not proceed on the legal or conventional rule in accordance with which the eldest, as distinct from the best qualified, inherits. Yet we can now distinguish between the direct rule of political wisdom, which is what we may call Lear's rule before the great eruption, and natural right proper. Lear's wise rule was still founded on opinion, as distinct from knowledge, and to that extent represented a kind of conventional right, albeit the best kind. We now see that Cordelia's precedence over her sisters is also a matter of natural right. But Cordelia's natural right to rule is not an element of political right. It follows, not from the wisdom of her father's choice, but from her intransigence in regard to truth.[35] Cordelia's natural right, far from being an element of political right, is destructive of political right. Lear's policy, which I have shown to be both wise and just, depends on a small hypocrisy, a relatively slight pretense. Cordelia's nature, refusing to make the concession that policy called for, reveals, at one and the same moment, its transcendent beauty and its superiority to, if not its contempt for, justice.[36]

It was Lear's intention that Cordelia become sovereign. That intention is fulfilled within the love test itself, but in a way that Lear did not anticipate. Nevertheless, we maintain, Cordelia does do what her father wishes her to do, but it is his unconscious wish that she fulfills. It requires the five acts of the tragedy for Lear to fully realize what that true wish was. Strangely enough, Lear, in his outburst against Cordelia, also acts in obedience to her, who is now his sovereign. In the region beyond that of the political, to which their relationship has now been transferred, the act of obedience, the act of the true subject, is the act of love. To command love in this nonpolitical sense means to cause loving in the soul of another. Cordelia can be the cause of that love which Lear's great soul needs only if Lear removes himself from, or removes from himself, every vestige of his monarchy in this world. We may summarize the ironies of Scene i by saying that the love test, which at first glance appears to be a straightforward demand for protestations of love, turns out to be an elaborately contrived deception; but the supreme deception is that of the deceiver himself, who really acts, in the final analysis, albeit unwittingly, for the very purpose for which he says he is acting. Lear, acting to discover the truth about his daughters' love, does what would have been foolish as a political action if it were not a pretense; yet it is not foolish in its deeper, nonpretending meaning, because it is no longer a political action, for Lear's action, but not Lear himself, is thoroughly rational in the rejection of Cordelia. Reason could not have devised a more straightforward way than that actually taken by Lear to divest himself of all the attributes of worldly monarchy.[37]

I have said that Cordelia's intransigent truthfulness showed her superiority, even to justice. It did, indeed, show that, on the level of political action, there need be no distinguishable difference between superiority to the claims of justice and rank injustice. This paradox, far from being merely apparent, is at the core of the tragedy of *King Lear* and lies in Shakespeare's vision of a universe in which the demands of justice are in an insoluble conflict with the demands of that truth which is, in its turn, the only unconditional motive for justice. The proposition that truth is the motive for justice is symbolized by the fact that Lear's entire policy—his wise and just policy—has as its foundation his conviction in regard to Cordelia. Yet it was impossible for Lear's conviction to be more than a mere opinion within the framework of that policy. Cordelia, responding to Lear's unconscious demand for truth, as distinct from mere opinion, compels him to act in the most unjust manner possible in order to discover that truth. Thus does the uncompromising quest for truth and love, which can be ultimately understood as different names for the same thing, destroy justice; even as the successful completion of Lear's original plan—while doing justice, that is, serving the common good—would forever have denied him that love and knowledge which alone could link his mighty soul to its source in eternity.

VI

In this incomplete and inadequate analysis of a single scene of a single play, I have attempted only a few hints at the range and precision of Shakespeare's analysis of the problematic character of the ultimate in human and political existence. No argument would have been needed to convince anyone of the breadth of the poet's vision of the human scene, but I think it indispensable to realize that there is a no less impressive intellectual precision underlying the amazing sweep. That precision is, I think, not an adventitious factor in the breadth, but its very condition. If there is a single philosophic doctrine which we may, without hesitation, ascribe to Shakespeare, it is that intellectual beauty is the condition of the existence of the beauty we apprehend with our senses. It would be an absurdity unworthy of his greatness to suppose that, though it was given him to move us with the images of the senses, as it has perhaps been given no other man to do, he was for this reason less concerned with the intellectual beauty which was its cause. This essay is intended to suggest that the vividness of the sensual world presented to us by Shakespeare is a pallid thing compared to that other world which was his ultimate concern.

In conclusion, I would apply this generalization to the political problem presented at the outset: the problem of the perpetuation of the perfect regime. Human life, we might say, is set in motion by the demands of human virtue. These demands require political life. But the full demands of virtue transcend political life. In a sense, they transcend human life. Lear, who is, after all, a mythical king of Britain, brought political life in the poet's own land to a peak that no actual king did. But the dynamism of Lear's soul, which drew the kingdom to this pitch, could not rest there. I said before that, according to Shakespeare, monarchy is the best form of government. This may now be qualified by saying that it is best only in a theoretical sense and, rather, that the understanding of monarchy, as the indispensable condition of the understanding of political life, is the condition of such actual perfection as may fall within our human compass. The understanding of monarchy is the condition of the understanding of the true relation of the political to the human and of the human to the divine. Surely, such knowledge was never more needful.

NOTES

1 See "The Perpetuation of Our Political Institutions," address before the Young Men's Lyceum of Springfield, Illinois, January 27, 1838. Compare Machiavelli, *Discourses on Livy*, I. x, where it is said that, not the founders of republics and monarchies deserve the greatest praise, but the founders of religions. One might paraphrase Machiavelli by saying that the founders of religions are the true founders of civil society; Numa, rather than Romulus, is the founder of Rome. Another expression of the same thought, which is classical as well as Machiavellian, is that to found a state is an act of human virtue, but to perpetuate it requires divine assistance. It is the thesis of this essay that Lear's incomprehension of this truth was his tragic flaw. It might not be irrelevant to add that Lincoln acted the role of high priest in the Civil War, a conflict which he interpreted, in his two most famous utterances, as a divine affliction, designed to transform a merely political union into a sacramental one.

2 Cf. A. C. Bradley, *Shakespearean Tragedy* (London: Macmillan, 1905), p. 243.

3 *Coleridge's Shakespearean Criticism*, ed. Thomas Middleton Raysor (Cambridge: 1930), Vol. I, p. 55, n. 1.

4 *Ibid.*, p. 59.

5 *Ibid.*, p. 226.

6 Bradley, *op. cit.*, p. 249.

7 *Loc. cit.*

8 *Ibid.*, p. 281.

9 *Ibid.*, p. 250.

10 Cf. Plato *Gorgias* 510^{B}2 ff.; Aristotle *Nicomachean Ethics* 1155^{a}33; Note 25, *infra*.

11 According to Wilfrid Perrett, *The Story of King Lear from Geoffrey of Monmouth to Shakespeare* (Berlin: 1904), p. 175, no earlier version of the play shows Goneril and Regan married before the love test. This accentuates Shakespeare's emphasis on the King's policy.

12 Cf. Tom Paine, *Rights of Man* (Everyman's Library), p. 51: "William the Conqueror and his descendants parcelled out the country in this manner, and bribed some parts of it by what they called charters to hold the other parts of it the better subjected to their will. This is the reason why so many of those charters abound in Cornwall; the people were averse to the Government established at the conquest, and the towns were garrisoned and bribed to enslave the country. All the old charters are the badges of this conquest, and it is from this source that the capriciousness of elections arises."

13 Crowns and coronets are distinguished from each other in a number of Shakespearean texts: *Henry V* II. Prologue. 11; *Tempest* I. ii. 133; *Julius Caesar* I. ii. 258. The crown is certainly one of the "additions to a king."

14 Compare Lear's apparent intention to resign authority to that of Charles V, a comparison that would have occurred readily to an Elizabethan audience. Charles had his son crowned in a great state ceremony, in his own presence, and in that same presence had all the great peers of his numerous realms pledge their fealty to Philip. He himself then retired to a monastery and remained virtually inaccessible to the political world. Lear, on the contrary, was to remain king, the sole bearer of regal authority. Living with Cordelia, he would remain at the center of political life. It is not merely the ancient habit of command that compels him, later in the play, to give orders to his daughters' retainers, but the evident assumption that his orders supersede all others. As I will attempt to show below, this assumption would not have been unreasonable if his *original* plan had been adhered to. In fact, Lear's altered plan ran athwart the whole feudal system, and in this respect his elder daughters had just grievance against him.

15 This was pointed out to me by Prof. R. S. Milne, Victoria University College, Wellington, New Zealand. Perrett, *op. cit.*, p. 153, says that it was for Cordelia. But why would a princess of the blood royal receive a coronet now?

16 Burgundy's reply to Lear's question as to "What, in the least" Burgundy will require in dowry to take Cordelia, is ambiguous: "Most royal majesty, I crave no more than hath your Highness offered." It is not certain whether Lear has already offered Cordelia herself to be bride to Burgundy, with the dowry of which Burgundy appears

to have knowledge, or whether Lear has simply informed Burgundy of the amount and kind of Cordelia's dowry.

[17] There does not seem to be any mention of Burgundy in Shakespeare's sources. He thus appears to be a Shakespearean addition, required to make possible Lear's original plan, as we are reconstructing it.

[18] To an Elizabethan audience, the Burgundian alliance would represent, in principle, the Spanish alliance, since Burgundy (or Franche-Comté) was part of the empire of Charles V and Philip II. A Spanish marriage would be in line with traditional English policy, as indicated by Henry VIII's marriage to a Spanish princess and his daughter Mary's marriage to Philip. Elizabeth, on the other hand, although she conducted a long and maddening flirtation with the Duke d'Alençon, never actually brought herself to a French marriage. Only the threat of a Franco-Spanish alliance against England could have led Elizabeth to indulge in her fabulously insincere and equally artful negotiations to become bride of the heir to the French throne. Elizabethan principles of power politics are clear enough. A smaller power, such as England, forms an alliance with a great but distant power, such as Spain, to neutralize such a great and near power as France. In like manner, Scotland's traditional ally was France: Scotland was to England as England to France; or, again, France was to Scotland as Spain to England.

[19] The legitimacy of Lear's rule, in the feudal sense of that term, is shrouded in the mist of the antiquity which surrounds the setting of the entire play. That the contemporary Elizabethan view of primogeniture is somehow present in Lear's legendary kingdom is indicated by Edmund's famous soliloquy in Scene ii and its sequel. All that need be said at the moment is that Lear is very old himself, his rule very successful, and his personal authority apparently unchallenged. But the obscurity of the legal foundation of the monarchy accentuates the political problem of the succession. Under traditional English rules, the eldest daughter would succeed in the absence of a male heir. Lear seems to be reversing that rule in making his youngest daughter his heir. But, if Lear's rule is just (until the fatal explosion), then it must be just in an extralegal sense, since he does not seem to be hampered—or guided—by any legal rules in deciding what is best. Lear's decision (as I believe) to make Cordelia his successor certainly seems right, since she alone of the daughters appears to inherit her father's regal qualities. Lear thus seems to act in the light of the truth—the truth that Cordelia is the best qualified—instead of in the conventional or legal expectation that the eldest should inherit. But a decision based on truth will be politically wise or truthful only if it is supported by public opinion. Lear's design—according to my interpretation—to cultivate the conditions for a public opinion favorable to his settlement is tantamount, then, to a design to provide a legal or conventional foundation for an arrangement which is, in its origin, essentially extralegal.

One might object, however, that public pledges without an underlying favorable distribution of power would be worthless, whereas, if such a distribution existed, the pledges would be superfluous. As suggested above, the pledges might themselves be an ingredient in the distribution of power. For example, consider such public pledges as Magna Carta. Magna Carta only affirmed what the barons present at Runnymede believed that they and the king already knew to be the law of the realm. Despite the fact that all must have believed that the king would in future, when he had power to do so, violate rights which he had disregarded in the past, it must also have been believed that his solemn public pledge would lessen his future power to do so. In like manner, we may suppose it possible that the pledges of Goneril and Regan may have served to minimize the opinion, particularly among their own followers, which might have been favorable to any attempt to upset Lear's will and testament.

20 They might have threatened Lear with a French alliance, just as Lear could threaten them with a French marriage for Cordelia.

21 Goneril: "He always loved our sister most"—I. i. 288. All citations are to the Furness variorum edition (Philadelphia: J. B. Lippincott Co., 1880).

22 E.g., Coleridge, *op cit.*, p. 54.

23 We are here concerned primarily with the way in which Lear marks the limits of human life by transcending them in the direction of the divine in his relationship with Cordelia. A full interpretation of the play would explain fully how Goneril and Regan mark the lower limits of humanity, passing beyond them into bestiality.

24 We must also give due weight to Lear's genuine paternal attachment to Goneril and Regan. It has been the thesis from the beginning that Lear was a political realist and estimated his daughters' merits without sentimentality. This does not mean, however, that he wished to think ill of any of them or that he had any inkling of the depths of baseness of Goneril and Regan. Lear's outburst against Cordelia was undoubtedly motivated, to some extent, by an instinctive awareness that Cordelia was tearing a veil that covered all their relationships, a veil on which were painted some pleasing illusions, illusions to which he was deeply attached even when not quite believing in them.

25 The tacit premise of this assertion is that we tend to resemble what we love. Cf. Plato *Gorgias* 510B2 ff. The principle is as follows: when we love someone, we praise what he praises and blame what he blames. But character is formed by responding to praise and blame, as a shoe is shaped on its last.

26 Compare the loveless plight of the tyrant in Xenophon's *Hiero* and the interpretation thereof in Leo Strauss's *On Tyranny* (New York: The Free Press of Glencoe, 1963).

27 We must not be blinded, by France's beautiful speech accepting Cordelia, to the prudential considerations which supported his action. To France, a claim on Cordelia's dowry, not to mention a claim on the British throne, was worth a good deal, whether acknowledged by Lear or not. France had forces to make good his claims, which Burgundy did not have. Hence, France could affect a generosity which Burgundy could not afford. Note that France parted from Lear "in choler," which is hardly the state of mind of a successful lover who

owes the success of his suit to the very temper of the old king which he now resents.

²⁸ This does not mean that, in a monarchy, one cannot obey the monarch and love justice without loving the monarch. One might regard the monarch's commands as just because they happen to conform to a nonmonarchical standard. Or one might recognize the monarchical principle as the highest one while holding the existing incumbent to be deficient in the qualities of a monarch. The second condition is not a genuine exception, because the regime would then not be monarchical in an unqualified sense. The fact that all actual monarchies may be nominal rather than real does not affect the argument. If, however, we consider the essence of monarchy, I believe the necessity for the statement in the text will appear. Monarchy is a political regime, consisting of a true king and true subjects. The true king is such by his pre-eminence in what his monarchical subjects recognize as virtue, as the true subjects are so by their obedience to the pre-eminent virtue of their ruler. But one cannot recognize virtue without loving it. Thus, the necessary and sufficient condition of the obedience of a *monarchical* subject is the love of the personage who embodies the ruling virtue. It is this kind of obedience alone which makes the regime essentially monarchical, and distinguishes it from other kinds of regimes.

²⁹ As long as his subjects believe that he has power, this belief is sufficient to produce the obedience which constitutes that power.

³⁰ Compare Lear with the good Duke Vincentio in *Measure for Measure*. The duke, in order to discover the truth about his subjects' characters, pretends to go on a long journey, delegating authority to some of those he wishes to test. He then returns disguised as a friar and becomes the confessor and spiritual adviser of several of the principals. This course is not open to Lear, for, among other things, he is king of a pre-Christian Britain. Another such comparison would be with Prospero in the *Tempest*. Prospero, however, has Ariel, and Ariel's power to produce illusions (according to Prospero's directions) makes the malefactors helpless to conceal their motives from the man who controls their access to reality. Neither Prospero nor Vincentio, however, although apparently exempted from Lear's "human" limitation of being unable to search men's hearts for their motives, is regal in the sense that Lear is. Both love "the life removed" and "the liberal arts"; neither is a truly political man. Neither, in fact, is a success as a ruler, because both neglect the duties of office for something they care for more.

³¹ Lear's later sense of the limitations of his former justice is shown in the famous lines on the heath:

> Take physic, pomp.
> Expose thyself to feel what wretches feel,
> That thou mayst shake the superflux to them
> And show the Heavens more just.
> III. iv. 33-36.

³² The best is an illusion because the virtue on which it is founded is an illusion. The tacit premise is, of course, that virtue is knowledge, but that Lear, deficient in the self-knowledge which the action of the tragedy alone could remove, did not achieve genuine knowledge and hence virtue until after he had ceased ruling. If the regime was constituted by the virtue of the ruler, ruling not only his subjects' actions but their hearts, then the regime, too, was, in this sense, an illusion.

³³ Compare *The Second Part of King Henry the Fourth* III. i. 6-33, the speech ending, "Uneasy lies the head that wears a crown," but especially Henry the Fifth's speech, in the play of that name, IV. i. 246-301:

> What infinite heartsease
> Must kings neglect that private men enjoy!
> And what have kings that privates have not too,
> Save ceremony, save general ceremony?

That is, kings are paid with an illusory good that their subjects may enjoy a real one.

³⁴ The connection between Lear's image of the world in which he is king and his image of the world in which he is no longer king is indicated in many ways, including the following. In Lear's curse, disinheriting Cordelia, as in his oath affirming the banishment of Kent, Lear thinks of the order of the universe as the work of living gods who are concerned with justice and injustice in the same sense in which he is concerned with them. When cursing Cordelia, he calls the light, the darkness, and "the orbs" from whose operation we both exist and cease to be to witness his disclaimer of "paternal care, propinquity and property of blood." But, if it is the operation of the divine order that is the cause of both our existence and nonexistence, Lear's belief that he could disclaim a connection determined by that order must mean that Lear believed that Cordelia, in offending her father, had offended that divine order and, in breaking links that connected her with her father in the local moral order, had broken the links connecting him with her in the supramundane, cosmic order. Similarly, Lear confirms the banishment of Kent with an oath "by Jupiter." The reference is to the king of the Olympian gods, Homer's father of gods and men, who is invoked as the substance of what is shadowy in Lear's authority.

If we now turn from Scene i to the great passion on the heath, we observe that Lear's consciousness of himself as a member of the imagined world he has until then inhabited culminates in his tearing off his clothes. The clothes, of course, represent the conventions which have hitherto concealed his true self from himself. Lear's next words after the "divesting" are in response to Kent's "How fares your Grace?" "What's he?" replies Lear, now unable or unwilling to recognize the conventional distinction implicit in the salutation. And Lear's very next words indicate how little of intentional irony there is in these lines. Gloucester is pleading with him to go in out of the storm. Lear demurs. "First let me talk with this philosopher." The person referred to is Edgar, disguised as a madman. "What is the cause of thunder?" demands Lear of the philosopher. Thus Lear, finally gone mad, as madness is understood in the world he has rejected, can no longer recognize the distinction of "grace," by which kings are kings, nor can he recognize in thunder the sign of Jupiter's authority, the authority which reinforces and guarantees the moral order represented in this world by kings. The thunderbolt, symbol of the power of Jupiter, has become a question of theoretical philosophy.

Finally, it is worth noting that Lear, alone of those present on the heath, penetrates Edgar's disguise, for Edgar is the philosopher who, at the last, provides the moral of the play. "Men must endure their going hence, even as their coming hither; ripeness is all" (V. ii. 9). Even this supreme insight has its irony, in that it is a truth conveyed by a son, Edgar, to his father, Gloucester. The catastrophe of the tragedy, its only catastrophe, is the catastrophe of that moral order to which Lear and Gloucester belonged when the play began—the moral order in which kings and fathers command, the moral order which is part of a larger order or cosmos, whose hierarchy maintains and is maintained by the kind of subordination and superordination implicit in the relationship of kings and subjects, fathers and sons. That the moral of the tragedy is expressed by Edgar and that his father must become his pupil to grow wiser is as much a part of the moral of the play as is the moral itself.

35 In short, Shakespeare would not accept Aristotle's formulation that natural right is a *part* of political right; *Nichomachean Ethics* 1134ᵇ18 ff. For Shakespeare, as for Plato, the highest form of political right reflects rather than embodies pure natural right. Natural right is distinguished from political right. It is a transcendental cause of political right, rather than an element in it. Cf. Leo Strauss, *Natural Right and History* (Chicago: University of Chicago Press, 1953), pp. 151-153.

36 We may here venture a hypothesis concerning one of the most difficult problems in the interpretation of *King Lear,* albeit one that goes beyond the proper scope of this essay. This is the problem of the ending—the apparent wantonness of the gods in permitting the deaths of Cordelia and Lear. It has been cited as a fundamental defect of the dramatic structure that these deaths do not follow as a result of the necessities of the action, as in the cases of Macbeth, Othello, Hamlet, Brutus, and other tragic heroes. It has been held that the poet's theme became too gigantic even for his colossal powers and that, although dramatic fitness required the deaths of the hero and heroine, he knew no way of effecting these deaths but by chance. I believe that there is another explanation.

One of the puzzles of the last scene is the apparently inexplicable delay of the dying Edmund, from Line 200, where he promises to "do good," until Line 245, where he finally tells of his order for the death of Cordelia. The delay might even conceivably be traced back to Line 163, where Edmund already appears to show remorse. The question is, Why, if Edmund's repentance is genuine, does he delay so long to tell of his order? The murder of Cordelia is the greatest of his crimes, and yet it lay within his power to stay the hand whose blow would put more guilt on him than any he had yet struck.

The solution, I believe, is this. The deaths of Lear and Cordelia were not matters of mere dramatic fitness. They were required as retribution for the transgressions against justice that both had committed. Both had sided with France against Britain. Lear's rejection of Cordelia was a blow at his own justice as king. Cordelia's invasion with French forces was not an act of public redress; it was motivated by love of her father, who was no longer the true king, because he had shown himself no longer capable of ruling. The defeat of the French forces and the unification of the kingdom under Albany is, we must observe, a political consummation which achieves all the just purposes of Lear's original plan. The survival of Lear and/or Cordelia would throw all this once more into confusion. Above all would this be true if Cordelia lived, for it would continue the French claims, the excuse for foreign intrusion. The dying Edmund means to do some good yet. What good, in the sense of justice, could he do better than to let the order against Cordelia's life run? It is necessary that Edmund remand the order as a way of showing his repentance for the merely malicious action he had heretofore done, but the silent delay shows a deeper understanding of the demands of justice, the demands that Cordelia, too, had rejected, in favor of something celestial, just as he had rejected them in favor of something infernal.

[37] The word "divest" is used advisedly. See Note 34, *supra*. When Lear reawakens, after the "divesting" in the storm scene, he is in Cordelia's arms, wearing different clothes, clothes that he does not recognize.

Acknowledgments

Chapter 2 originally appeared in *Social Research*, XXX (Spring 1963), No. 1, 1-22.

Chapter 3 originally appeared in *The American Political Science Review*, LIV (March 1960), No. 1, 129-157.

Chapter 5 originally appeared in *The American Political Science Review*, LI (June 1957), No. 2, 405-427.

Index

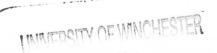

Lightning Source UK Ltd.
Milton Keynes UK
UKOW03f1450280317

297718UK00001B/19/P